JUAN DE VALDÉS
DON BENEDETTO

BECAUSE
of CHRIST

LIVING OUT THE C...
THROUGH FAI...

INTRODUCTION ..
LEON MORRIS
EDITED BY
JAMES M. HOUSTON

Victor®

The Bible Teacher's Teacher

COOK COMMUNICATIONS MINISTRIES
Colorado Springs, Colorado • Paris, Ontario
KINGSWAY COMMUNICATIONS
Eastbourne, England

Victor® is an imprint of
Cook Communications Ministries, Colorado Springs, CO 80918
Cook Communications, Paris, Ontario
Kingsway Communications, Eastbourne, England

BECAUSE OF CHRIST
© 2005 by James Houston
The Benefit of Christ
Copyright © 1984 by James M. Houston
Originally published 1984 by Multnomah Press, Portland, Oregon 92766.

Cover Design by: Jackson Design CO, LLC/Greg Jackson

First Victor Printing, 2005
Printed in the United States of America
1 2 3 4 5 6 7 8 9 10 Printing/Year 09 08 07 06 05

Unless otherwise noted, Scripture references in this volume are the original author's own translations. Other Scripture noted is taken from the Authorized (King James) Version of the Bible.

ISBN 0781441986
old ISBN: 1-55361-086-5 (Canada)
old ISBN: 1-57383-251-0 (United States)

Dr. James M. Houston was born to missionary parents who served in Spain. Dr. Houston served as University Lecturer at Oxford University, England, from 1949 to 1971. He was a Fellow of Hertford College during the period between 1964 and 1971, and held the office of Principal of Regent College from 1969 to 1978. He has served as Chancellor of Regent College and is currently Emeritus Professor of Spiritual Theology.

Dr. Houston has been active in the establishment and encouragement of lay training centers across the continents. These include the C. S. Lewis Institute in Washington, D.C., and the London Institute for the Study of Contemporary Christianity. In addition to his work with the classics series, he has published a book titled I Believe in the Creator *(Eerdmans, 1978).*

Other Victor Classics:
Faith Beyond Feelings, Jonathan Edwards
Triumph Over Temptation, John Owen
Watch Your Walk, Richard Baxter

CONTENTS

PART 1: THE EXPERIENCE OF JUSTIFICATION BY
FAITH: SELECTIONS FROM *ONE HUNDRED AND
TEN CONSIDERATIONS* AND OTHER WRITINGS
BY JUAN DE VALDÉS

PREFACE TO VICTOR CLASSICS

With the profusion of books now being published, most Christian readers require some guidance for a basic collection of spiritual works that will remain lifelong companions. This new series of Christian classics of devotion is being edited to provide just such a basic library for the home. Those selected may not all be commonly known today, but each has a central concern of relevance for the contemporary Christian.

Another goal for this collection of books is a reawakening. It is a reawakening to the spiritual thoughts and meditations of the forgotten centuries. Many Christians today have no sense of the past. If the Reformation is important to them, they jump from the apostolic Church to the sixteenth century, forgetting some fourteen centuries of the work of the Holy Spirit among many devoted to Christ. These classics will remove that gap and enrich their readers by the faith and devotion of God's saints through all history.

And so we turn to the books, and to their purpose. Some books have changed the lives of their readers. Notice how Athanasius's *Life of Antony* affected Augustine or William Law's *A Serious Call to a Holy Life* influenced John Wesley. Others, such as Augustine's *Confessions* or Thomas à Kempis's *Imitation of Christ*, have remained perennial sources of inspiration throughout the ages. We sincerely hope those selected in this series will have a like effect on our readers.

Each one of the classics chosen for this series is deeply significant to a contemporary Christian leader. In some cases, the thoughts and reflections of the classic writer are mirrored in the leader's genuine ambitions and desires today, an unusual pairing of hearts and minds across the centuries. And thus each individual has been asked to write the introduction on the book that has been so meaningful to his or her own life.

EDITING THE CLASSICS

Such classics of spiritual life have had their obstacles. Their original language, the archaic style of later editions, their length, the digressions, the allusions to bygone cultures—all make the use of them discouraging to the modern reader. To reprint them (as was done on a massive scale in the last century and still so today) does not overcome these handicaps of style, length, and language. To seek the kernel and remove the husk, this series involves therefore the abridging, rewriting, and editing of each book. At the same time we sought to keep to the essential message given in the work, and to pursue as much as possible the author's original style.

The principles of editing are as follows. Keep sentences short. Paragraphs are also shortened. Material is abridged where there are digressions or allusions made that are time-binding. Archaic words are altered. Spelling is that of *Webster's Dictionary* 11th Edition. Logical linkage may have to be added to abridged material. The identity of theme or argument is kept sharply in mind. Allusions to other authors are given brief explanation.

For the Christian, the Bible is the basic text for spiritual reading. All other devotional reading is secondary and should never be a substitute for it. Therefore, the allusions to Scripture in these classics of devotion are searched out and referenced in the text. This is where other editions of these books may ignore the scriptural quality of these works, which are inspired and guided by the Bible. The biblical focus is always the hallmark of truly Christian spirituality.

PURPOSE FOR THE CLASSICS: SPIRITUAL READING

Since our sensate and impatient culture makes spiritual reading strange and difficult for us, the reader should be cautioned to read these books slowly, meditatively, and reflectively. One cannot rush through them like a detective story. In place of novelty, they focus on remembrance, reminding us of values that remain of eternal consequence. We may enjoy many new things, but values are as old as God's creation.

The goal for the reader of these books is not to seek information. Instead, these volumes teach one about living wisely. That takes obedience, submission of will, change of heart, and a tender, docile spirit. When John the Baptist saw Jesus, he reacted, "He must increase, and I must decrease." Likewise, spiritual reading decreases our natural instincts, to allow His love to increase within us.

Nor are these books "how-to" kits or texts. They take us as we are—that is, as persons, and not as functionaries. They guide us to "be" authentic, and not necessarily to help us to promote more professional activities. Such books require us to make time for their slow digestion, space to let their thoughts enter into our hearts, and discipline to let new insights "stick" and become part of our Christian character.

—James M. Houston

EDITOR'S NOTE ON THE CLASSICS OF VALDÉS AND BENEDETTO

It may come as something of a surprise to many of us that Italy produced one of the clarion statements about justification by faith during the sixteenth century.

We do not think of Italy as participating in the Reformation. In fact, we think of Italy as a bastion of the Roman Church with its Popes acting as both civil and ecclesiastical rulers. How is it, then, that Italy was deeply penetrated by thought so close to the Protestant Reformers?

Indeed, it is not commonly realized that the Papal Representative at the Colloquy of Ratisbon in 1541, Cardinal Contarini, actually agreed with the Reformers previously on the doctrine of justification by faith.[1] When he died the following year, his successor Carafa was an intransigent, conservative Catholic, who reorganized the Inquisition in Italy in 1542. He purposed to stamp out the reforming spirit which he saw threatening the papacy.

But Carafa's suspicions were aroused too late. For the chief apostle of justification by faith in Italy, Juan de Valdés, died in 1541. It was he who had inspired the faith of many influential churchmen and scholars in Italy. It looked as if there was actually crypto-Lutheranism within Rome itself. Rather scornfully Calvin alluded to this movement within Italy in 1543 as "Nicodemite," an allusion to Nicodemus as a secret disciple of Jesus.[2] It was a faith not for public knowledge. But what else could its adherents have done? One could flee into exile, as Peter Martyr and Bernardino Ochino, Captain

General of the Capuchin Order, did in 1541. Or else one could choose to be tried and suffer martyrdom as Cardinal Carnesecchi and Aonio Paleario, among others, did later.

THE IMPORTANCE TODAY OF THESE WORKS

We ought still to be challenged and refreshed by these works. For they are two basic works of Italian Reformation thought, possibly the most important works that we shall ever have. They protest not merely against the corruptions of the Roman Church of that time as Luther did, but they are also a challenge to the Italian humanism of the Renaissance; such was never encountered by Luther.

In this latter respect, these works speak therefore much more to our own times and mind-set. Indeed, the irony of today's times is our boast as Evangelicals of holding high the doctrine of justification by faith. Yet it is increasingly apparent that the post-Vatican II spiritual directors seem to know more of the existential reality of grace as a lived experience than we do. It is they who are teaching evangelical leaders about a deeper spirituality than what is often exhibited in their evangelical leadership.

The majority of Evangelicals seem to live today with the secular assumption that function determines being. "What we do determines who we are." Workaholism and activism become the standard response. Many a Catholic retreat center today provides a tranquil haven and a new sense of evangelical grace that we woefully lack. It is the evangelical world itself which needs to be brought back to recover its own rich heritage in the biblical and reformed truth of justification by faith. This anthology is presented, then, as a timely work to encourage, as well as to challenge, our secularized evangelicalism.

Calvin's *Institutes* richly and effortlessly teaches us the full doctrine of atonement by faith. The *Considerations* of Juan de Valdés reflects more of a struggle and debate among a group of friends about how the experience of justification by faith is actually lived and thought. Valdés prepared these 110 "considerations" as topics for discussion with his friends while picnicking each Sunday in the countryside outside Naples. They covered the period 1536–41. Here, then, we have living documents exemplifying Valdés's own deep conviction that Christian doctrine can never be considered theoretically; it must always be experienced as well as known mentally.

It was the reformed hermeneutical approach, the emphasis on the guidance and presence of the Holy Spirit, and thus the recovery of biblical truth, regardless of tradition, that helped the Italian movement recognize "The Benefit of Christ's Death." Others in Germany might speak of "Lutheranism," or of "Calvinism" in Geneva, but here in Italy the watchword was "Il Beneficio di Christo." The anonymous treatise of that title that was attributed to Don Benedetto and published two years after the death of Valdés is an important document summing up the whole spirit of this reformed movement.

But how did it all arise in Italy? Clearly it was both a reaction to Italian humanism as well as a reform of a worldly and corrupt church. It was also the recovery of biblical thought by men reading the Pauline epistles in the original language. But above all, it was the personal influence of Juan de Valdés (c. 1498–1541), who led a distinguished career as courtier, scholar, politician, and theologian.

THE LIFE AND THOUGHT OF JUAN DE VALDÉS

Juan de Valdés was the son of a Spanish nobleman whose brother was private secretary to Charles V, Emperor of the Holy Roman Empire. Juan was educated at the new university of Alcalá near Madrid which focused attention on biblical studies. Before that formal education, a Franciscan reformer, Alcaraz, had introduced Juan to the Bible, and especially to Pauline thought.

Both Alcaraz and Valdés belonged for a number of years to the same household of the Marques de Villena at Escalona. Both became "Alumbrados," and both were tried by the Spanish Inquisition. Alcaraz was earlier condemned and imprisoned in 1524, but Valdés was released on the recommendation of his professors at Alcalá in 1529.[3] His publication, *The Dialogue of the Christian Doctrine*, had already urged that the church needed reform. With the threat of a second trial by the Inquisition, Valdés fled in 1531 to Italy.[4]

What followed his flight were the most fruitful years of his life. Living in Naples between 1536 and his death in 1541, he wrote a number of books to instruct his close friend, the widow Guilia Gonzaga. *The Spiritual Alphabet* (c. 1536) was the first evangelical manifesto to be published in Italy to proclaim the doctrine of justification by faith. There followed four Bible commentaries: *On Romans* (c. 1536), *First Corinthians* (c. 1539), *The First Book of Psalms* (c. 1536), and *Matthew* (c. 1541). Excerpts of these have been included in this anthology.

CX Divine Considerations was compiled about 1540. Kept by Guilia Gonzaga after Valdés's death, it was eventually taken by Vergerio, bishop of Capo d'Istria, to Basel where it was published in 1550. Later it was translated and published in Lyons (1565), in Paris (1567), in Amsterdam (1565), and in Oxford and Cambridge (1646). Nicholas Ferrar translated it into English, while his friend George Herbert revised its style.

The following rewritten selections of this work are based upon the text of John T. Betts which was published in 1865.[5] Since then only the first ten "Considerations" have been republished in English.[6] So this is the fullest reprint of the material since the middle of the last century.

The interest of Valdés's *Considerations* is that there is no evidence he or his circle of friends were in touch with the Reformation sources of Luther, Calvin, or other works in the 1530s. Yet later at the trial of Valdés's friend Cardinal Carnesecchi before the Inquisition, the Inquisition judge saw no distinction between Lutheranism and Valdés's teaching.

Valdés saw clearly that the natural man, by natural knowledge, cannot fulfill his own ideals because of the depravity caused by original sin. He also saw that scriptural knowledge alone, without the Spirit of God, is still a form of natural knowledge. The only knowledge that man can have for salvation is that which he finds in Christ.

By this Valdés means that the consciousness of sin, the grace of the Gospel, and the rule of the Holy Spirit within the life of the believer are necessary. Thus the Holy Scriptures by themselves, without the illumination of the Holy Spirit, are not a source of proper knowledge of God.

Moreover, Valdés says that the Holy Spirit is identical with the Spirit of Christ; He has Christ's own mind and emotions. Without the Spirit of Christ, no exegesis of the text, no exhaustive grammatical understanding is enough. So in his *Commentary on Matthew,* Valdés emphasizes, "The Scriptures, written with the Holy Spirit, have also to be interpreted with the same Spirit with which they were written." The Holy Spirit as the Originator of the Scriptures is also the Master of its interpretation. Only the mind inspired by the Holy Spirit can read the Bible validly.

Valdés also emphasizes the central importance of personal Christian experience. The Christian faith is not a theoretical system but a lived reality. "Consider," the verb used by Valdés for his title "Divine Considerations," means that type of reflective knowledge based on experience and observation of the ways of God. This knowledge belongs to the experience of the Holy Spirit in one's life, so he says explicitly in *Considerations* that "all men who are without the Holy Spirit are without experience in spiritual and divine things." The Christian life is a deepening of experience and knowledge at the same time when one depends solely upon the grace of God. Such experience then is the gift of God through faith.

Thus the doctrine of atonement is central to Valdés's work. He saw—independently of Luther—that God's justice is truly understood only when seen in the light of Christ's death. For there the justice and goodness of God meet. It is the execution of God's judgment upon Christ that is man's assurance he will not be judged again. Christ has been our substitute. The Cross satisfies God's justice as it assures man of mercy.

Valdés also introduced the doctrine of justification into the Italian and Spanish worlds for the first time.[7] By justification he meant the new state man has before God because of Christ's death on man's behalf. It is based upon faith as trust in God's work of mercy. It is also based upon hope that generates love. Thus all that a man receives from God in the person and work of God is "the benefit of Christ."

Justification is one aspect of this benefit. It is demonstrable, however, in the spiritual progress the believer makes in being dead to the world and alive unto Christ. For Valdés, justification, regeneration, and sanctification are all one continuous assurance the Christian has in his own experience of being united with Christ. It is all a new life. Good works will follow as fruit is produced by the roots of that tree.

What is clear is that Valdés's experience of grace shatters all human efforts at self-justification and religious self-fulfillment. Salvation is the restoration of the divine image in man by Christ; it is wholly the work of God. That is why it is also the glory of God for man to be blessed and for man to grow in the grace of God.

In Valdés we find echoes of the later thought of Pascal. Both men reject the rationalistic strain in Protestantism and of scholastic theology generally. Valdés sets illumination of the mind by the Holy Spirit in opposition to theological rationalism. After his death, his thought was viewed as "Protestant"; yet his was no political motive but a personal longing for inner spiritual reform. He propagated no "school," and his pastoral care of his friends, such as Guilia Gonzaga, showed soul-friendship of the highest integrity. He demonstrates to us today that biblical truth requires no denominational framework, no political institution, and no ecclesiastical structure for its preservation. It can be expressed simply in the experience of a man and his intimate circle of friends.

The emphasis Valdés placed on personal experience of doctrine and of the reality of the Holy Spirit operative in one's own life is best summarized in a letter he wrote to a friend.

"When a man studies the books of others, he becomes acquainted with the mind of the authors, but not with his own mind. Yet it is the duty of a Christian to learn to know himself, to know his condition as a child of God through Christian regeneration. So I believe it is necessary for a Christian to be his own book. I believe that it is my mind that is my own book, because here are held false and true beliefs. Here I can discover my confidence and diffidence, my faith and unbelief, my hope and negligence, my love and hate ... indeed, my own self-love. At times I enter into a very strict account with myself and examine how far I love God and Christ. ... This is the way I study my OWN BOOK. The result of all this perusal is that I am able to reach a much better knowledge of what I am, and of what I am in myself, and what I am in and through God and Christ. And so I arrive at a more intimate knowledge of the *benefit to be received from Christ*. And this is the result, that the more constantly I read this book of mine, the more life I realize that I have in the grace of God and Christ, who grows in me more and more, and so the less of a son of Adam I become."[8]

DON BENEDETTO'S BENEFIT OF JESUS CHRIST CRUCIFIED

If the *Considerations* is Valdés's most mature theological thought, Benedetto's *Benefits* goes further. Benedetto sees the acceptance of the doctrine of justification as so central to Christian faith that those who reject it cannot be considered to be true Christians. He therefore abandoned the ideal of a unified Christian world that was represented by one's church.

Consequently, Benedetto shifted toward an invisible society of the elect that was composed of true Christians, justified by faith, and guided by the Spirit of Christ. He sees this true church existing side by side with the moral abyss and schisms of the historical church, which contained both true and false Christians. Indeed, he saw the true Christians as a minority within organized religion. Yet Benedetto also believed that many pious adherents of Rome would surely have their eyes opened to the truth in reading his book.

We know nothing of the man Don Benedetto who wrote this

wonderful book on Christian assurance. Indeed, until recent times, the work was attributed to Aonio Paleario (1503–1570), who was condemned by the Inquisition and burnt as a martyr.[9] He too had acknowledged writing a book entitled the *Benefit of Christ*.[10] No copy of his work has survived. But it is the testimony of Cardinal Carnesecchi before the Inquisition that identifies Benedetto. He acknowledged he had read Benedetto's manuscript in Naples. It was later revised by the poet Flaminio, possibly in Carnesecchi's home in Florence. It was then published in Venice in 1543 and put on the Index in 1549.

It appears that Don Benedetto was a Benedictine monk of Mantua in northern Italy. He took his vows there in 1519. Later, when he lived in Venice, he became a close friend of Flaminio. Flaminio in turn was a good friend of Juan de Valdés. In 1537 Don Benedetto was transferred to a monastery in Catania, Sicily, called Nicola all'Arena. Benedetto died there in 1544, a year after his book was published. It is likely that he visited the circle at Naples more than once, but we do not know what his personal links were with Juan de Valdés, although the testimony of Caracciolo before the Inquisitors was that Benedetto was "a friend of Valdés." But the book echoes the thought of the *Considerations*.

Although the circumstances surrounding the completion of the *Beneficio* remain obscure, its ready acceptance in the Protestant world is well known. It was translated into French in 1552, into English in 1573, into German, and even into Croatian. The text used here was rewritten on the basis of the edition of J. Ayre, published in 1851. I have also consulted the new English translation of the Italian text by Ruth Prelowski (1965).[11]

Benedetto sometimes paraphrases or adds his own interpretation to the biblical quotations. These have been rendered consistent in quoting from the Authorized version of the Bible. Paragraphs and subtitles have been added to his text to assist the reader. The full text of Benedetto's work has been incorporated.

No one is better qualified as a theologian of the Cross than Dr.

Leon Morris. We are grateful he has written the Introduction and critique of Benedetto's classic, a work which is perhaps the climax of Reformed thought in sixteenth-century Italy.

—James M. Houston

NOTES

[1] Philip McNair, *Peter Martyr in Italy, An Anatomy of Apostasy* (Oxford: Clarendon, 1967), 15.

[2] Ibid., 6.

[3] Jose C. Nieto, *Juan de Valdés and the Origins of the Spanish and Italian Reformation* (Geneva: Droz, 1970), 65–80.

[4] See J. E. Longhurst, *Erasmus and the Spanish Inquisition: The Case of Juan de Valdés* (Albuquerque, N.M.: University Press of New Mexico, 1950).

[5] B. B. Wiffen, *Life and Writings of Juan de Valdés* (London: Bernard Quaritch, 1865).

[6] George Hunstanton Williams and Angel M. Mergal, eds., *Spiritual and Anabaptist Writers* (London: S.C.M. Press, 1957), 335–350.

[7] See excellent summary of Valdés's theological thought in Nieto, *Juan de Valdés*, 185–337.

[8] Wiffen, *Life and Writings*, 177–178.

[9] Reverend John Ayre, ed., *The Benefit of Christ's Death; of the Glorious Riches of God's Free Grace Which Every True Believer Receives by Jesus Christ, and Him Crucified*. Originally written in Italian, but now reprinted from an ancient English translation (London: Religious Tract Society, 1847, 1851).

[10] Salvatore Caponnetto, *Aonio Paleario e La Riforma Protestante in Toscana* (Turin: Claudiana Editrice, 1979).

[11] Ruth Prelowski, "The Beneficio di Christo," in *Italian Reformation, Studies in Honour of Laelius Socinus*, edited by John A. Tedeschi (Florence: Monnier, 1965).

INTRODUCTION

Juan de Valdés and Don Benedetto were Italian Reformers. This comes as something of a surprise to most of us, for we do not think that the Reformers and Italy go together. When we think of the Reformation, we tend to think of it as a northern phenomenon. We have in mind Luther and Calvin, Scandinavia and the English Reformers. Few of us include Italy. We know that there were a few bold spirits there like Savanarola, but basically we see Italy as a bastion of Roman Catholicism.

There is some basis for the sentiment about northern Europe and the Reformation, but we should not overlook the fact that the people of southern Europe were not untouched by the powerful currents of thought that swept through many lands. The corruptions in the life of the church that caused such an upheaval in the north were not unknown in the south; in Italy, as elsewhere, there were many who were dissatisfied with medieval Roman Catholicism. There were movements of dissent, and, in reaction, movements of repression. There was tumult and uncertainty.

In Italy life was complicated by the number of small states with their jealousies and rivalries and with the constant intervention of the great powers. Some of the petty rulers were very conservative and enforced the papal will with rigor. Others were more open to new ideas and allowed a measure of dissent. Sometimes one type of ruler was replaced by one of the other type; this complicated life for those they ruled.

In Italy the course of those troubled days was different from that farther north. The Pope was a temporal ruler as well as the spiritual head of the church. He was much closer at hand than he was to the northerners, and he was supported by hordes of friars and others in the church.

In Italy there was much stronger opposition to the new thinking. That did not mean that such thought did not make its appearance. It did, and some of the dissatisfied could be very radical. They could even call in question such a central doctrine as the Trinity. But the Pope was stronger here than he was farther north, and in due time the Protestant movement ceased to be of any great importance.

But we should not overlook the fact that there were some significant figures associated with the Reformation in Italy as elsewhere. Included among them were people such as Juan de Valdés, Aonio Paleario, Peter Martyr Vermigli, Don Benedetto, and others. Out of this circle came a veritable ferment of new thinking as is clear from the *Considerations* of Valdés and from the little book entitled *The Benefit of Christ, Crucified* by Don Benedetto. As the editor has already introduced the works of Valdés, it is the volume by Don Benedetto to which we will now turn our attention.

The Benefit of Christ, Crucified was published in Venice in 1543, and 40,000 copies were reputed to have been sold before 1549. It speedily aroused opposition, for a Dominican monk wrote to confute it in 1544. It was put on the Index of prohibited books in 1549 at Venice. It was also printed in other places; Modena is known to have had a reprint. Vergerio, who had been bishop of Capo D'Istria, wrote notes on the books on the Index and he speaks warmly of *The Benefit of Christ, Crucified*. He says that two people were involved in it, one having written it and the other having revised it.

The book was popular enough for translations to be made into French, Slavonic, and German. In due course an English translation appeared, and later a further English edition, this one translated from the French. This second translation went through quite a number of editions. Despite this the book has been little known in recent times, and it is very difficult to obtain a copy. So it is good to have this new English edition.

Don Benedetto was clearly at home in Reformed theology. He was sure of the importance of the Bible, and, while he makes significant references to the works of the Fathers, his constant appeal to Scripture shows where he found that authority lay. He was clear that the Cross is of central importance, as the title of his book shows. The Reformation crux, justification by faith, he had clearly made his own, and he is unwearied in his reiteration of this doctrine. He emphasizes the significance of the Cross and dwells on it. He is equally sure of the importance of saving faith and gives a good deal of attention to what this means. There cannot be the slightest doubt of his commitment to the great doctrines emphasized at the Reformation.

His book majors on the Cross, the great central doctrine of Christianity. Paul could write, "we preach Christ crucified" (1 Cor. 1:23), where his language points to the habitual practice. He means that the atoning work of the crucified Savior is at the heart of the Christian message. That was what the Christians were always preaching. And this was no personal idiosyncrasy of Paul's, for he writes to the Corinthians, "whether it were I or they, so we preach, and so you believed" (1 Cor. 15:11). This central doctrine is always at the heart of authentic Christian preaching.

It is an inexhaustible topic. That Christ's death is central, in the literal sense of the term "crucial," is plain. How it accomplishes our salvation is not. Thus the church's thinkers have grappled with the problem over the centuries, and there is still no agreed solution. I write freely on this, for I have contributed five books to the never-ending stream and know that I have but scratched the surface.

I have been connected with Christian things all my life. In childhood I went to church and Sunday school as so many of us did, and again as is too common, largely as a matter of form. There was no sense of being gripped by the wonder of God's love, only a performance of certain duties.

During my undergraduate days all that changed. I was brought to think seriously about the Christian faith. I met people for whom the Christian way was no formality, but an absorbing way of life. Faith in Christ was for them not simply so many words, but an attitude that governed everything. I came to see that Christ must be central to all of life or there is no point in referring to Him as "Jesus Christ our

Lord" at all. And the commitment made then has affected all of my life ever since.

But commitment does not mean the end of questions. Indeed, in a sense it begins them. What was once a conventional, rather dull, unexciting, and undemanding part of life was transformed into a fascinating and far-from-obvious center of everything. Why should Christianity have a cross at its center? It became an intriguing mental quest as well as a satisfying and fulfilling way of life. I came to see that God's saving act is the central thing and that everything depends on that act. But how?

How does God's loving act save? How can the death of Jesus on Calvary's cross so many centuries ago save me now?

The conventional answers were not sufficient. They brought a measure of illumination, it is true. Christ paid the price, He bore the penalty, He won the victory, He set the example, He revealed the love of God. But no one of them is all the truth. And if we say we must combine them all, it is not immediately obvious how we can put them together. We learn something from the Synoptists, something from John, something from Paul, something in fact from every New Testament writer. But we cannot put their writings into one system. And none of them ever sets himself to answer the question, "How?" Through the centuries Christian theologians have grappled with the question, and we gain enlightenment by wrestling with their thought, even if in the end we must feel that none has given us the definitive answer.

The quest goes on. And the fact that there seems little hope that anyone will ever come up with the complete and perfect answer is not in the least daunting. For the fact is that the quest is rewarding in itself. Every tiny piece of truth we learn brings us so much closer to the Savior. The more I know about the Cross, the more the Cross comes to mean to me. And the more the Cross comes to mean to me, the richer becomes the salvation Christ won for me there. So I must go on. The author of *Benefits* surely felt something like this as he progressed from his formal Christian upbringing to his book about the Cross.

Why should we go back to a work written as long ago as 1543? Why not content ourselves with more up-to-date treatments of the topic? Basically because this little work is a classic and we can still learn from it. But it was written for other times and other people and it may help the modern reader if we notice some general considerations about its argument.

The book is arranged logically and begins with a study of original sin. It is of interest that Benedetto sees man in his original creation not only "as touching his soul, righteous, true, good, merciful, and holy," but also "in respect of his body, impassible" (p. 1, John Ayre edition, 1851). His idea that the body of Adam was incapable of suffering is arresting, and one not much discussed in modern times. It appears to be a deduction from the biblical statement that man was made in the image of God. There is no positive evidence for it, but it was held firmly by some; for example, A. H. Strong tells us that Albertus Magnus taught that "the first man would have felt no pain, even though he had been stoned with heavy stones."[1] That Adam was physically perfect was widely taught.

For Benedetto, the important thing about Adam was not, however, his interesting physical constitution, but the fact that his sin had calamitous consequences for the whole race, for "our whole nature was corrupted by Adam's sin" (p. 8, Ayre ed.). He thinks that it is important to be clear about this right at the beginning, for nobody will come to Christ without realizing that he is a sinner.

A further preliminary is a consideration of the place of the law. This was an outworking of God's compassion, and was sent to make people understand their position as sinners. The author discerns what he calls the five "offices" of the law: First, like a looking glass, it is to show a man what he is like; second, it is to make sin increase; third, it is to show the wrath and the judgment of God; fourth, it is "to put a man in fear"; while its fifth and principal office is to constrain him "to go unto Christ" for salvation.

It arises from this that the law cannot bring salvation, and Benedetto insists on this. All works of the law are "hurtful" (p. 24, Ayre ed.), and it is a "thing abominable" to try to justify ourselves (p. 22, Ayre ed.). But his consideration of original sin and of the place of the law is a necessary preliminary, for "he shall never know what is sweet, who hath not tasted of the sour" (p. 16, Ayre ed.). But we must not be too depressed at these preliminaries, for we cannot hold that the sin of Adam was of more force than the righteousness of Christ, a thought that Benedetto repeats (pp. 17, 19, Ayre ed.). Christ brings forgiveness, justification, salvation—express it how you will.

Our author does not really grapple with the problem of how the death of Christ so many years ago can save people now. Perhaps it is asking too much to look for such a discussion at that time. It is a question that has been given a good deal of attention in more recent times with no general agreement remotely in sight. At the Reformation there was no question about Christ being our Savior; the question was how good works relate to the salvation He brings, whether justification required any other condition from the human side than faith. It is enough for Benedetto that Christ has done all that is necessary for our salvation. He does not really grapple with the "how" of it at all.

What he does do is to emphasize certain important truths. He does not hesitate to use the concept of punishment and speaks of God as punishing Christ for our sins (pp. 20, 30–31, 35, 82, 93, Ayre ed.), and he uses vivid language as when he speaks of God as "punishing, chastising, and whipping His only-begotten and dear beloved Son instead of us" (p. 93, Ayre ed.). Most modern writers hesitate to speak of Christ as being "punished"; if they are speaking of this aspect of the atonement, they usually prefer to say that He bore our penalty or something like that. Benedetto had no such inhibitions. He has his own individual way of putting it, but he is here giving expression to a facet of the atonement that was important to most of the Reformers. It is out of favor in many modern discussions, but it does draw attention to one aspect of New Testament teaching. His discussion is all the more important accordingly.

Our author is especially fond of the idea that believers are clothed with the righteousness of Christ, and he returns to this again and again. This had, of course, become part of the conventional way of expressing our salvation, though few of us realize that "the righteousness of Christ" is not a New Testament expression at all. There we read of "the righteousness of God" (Rom. 1:17; 3:21–26; 10:3; 2 Cor. 5:21), and of righteousness as being reckoned to us (Rom. 4:3, 6, etc.), and of righteousness as being by faith (Rom. 9:30; 10:6). Perhaps the difference is not great, but it should be recognized if we are to be completely scriptural in our understanding of Christ's atonement.

We might deduce something like "the righteousness of Christ" from what is undoubtedly a scriptural truth, namely that believers are "in Christ." If we are "in" Him, then it may be legitimate to say that we are "clothed" by Him or by His righteousness, though this is rarely done. I am not trying to criticize the author, for his expression is one often used by the Reformers and their descendents, and one that has passed unquestioningly into accepted Christian vocabulary. I am doing no more than saying that that is not the way the New Testament expresses it, and that in my opinion it is better to use the New Testament expression, "the righteousness of God."

Ever since the appearance of Aulen's book *Christus Victor*, it has been fashionable to stress the importance of the note of victory. Christ not only paid the penalty and set the example; He won a resounding victory over all the forces of evil. Benedetto is clear on this note of victory. Believers are free from the law, sin, and death (p. 26, Ayre ed.); they have overcome sin, death, the Devil, and hell (p. 27, 29, Ayre ed.); they have no fear of death, sin, the Devil, and hell (p. 99, Ayre ed.). It is an important part of the Atonement that Christ has won the victory, and we must be grateful to men such as our author for their emphasis on this great truth.

One of God's good gifts in Christ which has not been so much stressed is the sheer joy that results from Christ's dealing with our sins. To be a sinner is to be lost; to be in Christ is to be saved, and that is a wonderfully joyful experience. The New Testament is full of the note of joy. The words *joy* and *rejoice* occur not infrequently, but there are several other words which do not give English readers the appearance of having anything to do with joy, but which are derived ultimately from the same Greek root. For example, grace (*charis*) means "that which causes joy (*chara*)"; you can hear the one word in the other. It is the same with one of the words for "forgive" (*charizomai*); the element of joy in forgiveness should not be overlooked. Then there is the word in common use these days, *charisma*, which is simply the Greek word taken over and made part of our language. *Charismatic* is, of course, derived from this and likewise contains the note of joy.

Joy runs through and through the New Testament, but theologians for the most part have muted this happy note. As C. S. Lewis puts it in the title of his autobiography, they are "Surprised by Joy." Not so Benedetto. One of the things I very much like about his approach to the subject is his stress on the joy of the Christian. This is big in the New Testament, and unfortunately small in the experience of some believers. There is no question but that it is a most important part of the Christian way for our Reformer.

"Let us live merrily," he writes, "and assured that the righteousness of Jesus Christ has utterly done away all our unrighteousness" (p. 28, Ayre ed.); trust in God's mercy "enlarges our heart, cheers it up" (p. 39, Ayre ed.); we do good works "with a certain liveliness and effectual cheerfulness" (p. 40, Ayre ed.); faith in Christ "cheerfully destroys and overthrows the Devil" (p. 56, Ayre ed.); the man that knows himself righteous through Christ "labours happily" (p. 60, Ayre ed.); faith makes us enjoy pardon and maintains us "in continual joy" (p. 58, Ayre ed.); faith in Christ "makes men true Christians, stout, cheerful, merry …" (p. 74, Ayre ed.); "happy is that man that … will neither hear nor see any other thing than Jesus Christ crucified" (p. 93, Ayre ed.); predestination, far from being the grim doctrine that some have made it, "maintains the true Christian in a continual spiritual joy" (p. 99, Ayre ed.). The author speaks of "the spiritual cheerfulness and joy, which is peculiar to the Christian" (p. 112, Ayre ed.); he reminds his readers that Paul "does oftentimes encourage the Christian to live merrily" (p. 113, Ayre ed.). Theologians as a race tend to be solemn folk, and it is good to see this emphasis on the sheer merriment of being Christian. We are indifferent theologians if we have lost the song in the heart.

The author has a long chapter (as long as any in his book) headed "Of the Effects of Lively Faith, and of the Union of Man's Soul with Jesus Christ" (chapter 11). It is clearly this that grips him. Christ's death has provided the means of our salvation, and this means an end to all works of law, all attempts to win salvation by our own efforts. But that does not mean that all are saved. It is important that we put our trust in Christ, and when we do, all the benefits of Christ's death flow into our lives.

The author makes much of the biblical figure of marriage and uses it sometimes in ways that seem quaint to our manner of thinking. But his approach is stimulating, and it is useful to have our horizons stretched by seeing how a man in a very different time and a very different place viewed this aspect of Christian teaching. He points out that the goods of a married couple become common to them both: The husband speaks of the wife's dowry as his, while the wife calls the husband's house and all his riches hers. Now God has "married his only-begotten and dear beloved Son to the faithful soul" (p. 30, Ayre ed.). The result is that Christ has full possession of the believer's "peculiar dowry," namely sin. The author spells this out: The dowry comprises "her sins and transgressions of the law, God's wrath against her, the boldness of the Devil over her, the prison of hell, and all other of her evils" (p. 30, Ayre ed.). The other side of this coin, of course, is that the wife of Christ receives "His holiness, His innocency, His righteousness, and His Godhead, together with all His virtue and might" (p. 31, Ayre ed.).

This is a compelling and powerful figure. The author goes on to the thought that "all the works of either of them" are "common to them both" (p. 32, Ayre ed.). It is possible to think that he goes further than Scripture in working out the implications of this way of looking at salvation, but there is no doubt about his central point, that union with Christ has far-reaching effects.

Faith is the significant thing. Benedetto knows that there are humble, hesitant Christians who find difficulty in appropriating the riches Christ has won for them. He refers to people who might readily think of other believers as "queen and mistress of his great riches" (p. 34, Ayre ed.), but who lack the assurance for themselves. What is the answer to their difficulty? "True and lively faith." For Benedetto it is impossible to overemphasize the importance of faith from the human side. We can bring nothing in the way of works; we bring nothing but our sins. But faith opens up the way into the fullness of the blessing. None should "distrust in himself," fearing that what Scripture says does not belong to him (p. 37, Ayre ed.); what Scripture says it says to all.

The point matters. Benedetto brings out its importance with another illustration, that of a king who offers pardon to rebels. Everyone who accepts the pardon can return to his own home and enjoy living "under the shadow of that holy king" (p. 37, Ayre ed.). But if he does not return, he bears the penalty. Unbelief means accounting God a liar and deceiver, and shuts us out from the blessing. Again we see the importance of faith.

There has always been a tendency to see something of a difficulty in the relationship between faith and works. Wherever the truth is grasped that "nothing in my hand I bring, simply to thy cross I cling," wherever it is seen that our best efforts cannot bring us salvation and that salvation is received as a free gift from God, there is a tendency to say, "Then works do not matter." The attitude has always been there; it goes back to the time of Paul (Rom. 6:1, 15).

But our author will have none of it. For him faith is active. No sooner is true faith given to a man (it is not a human achievement, but a gift of God) than he is "imprinted with a certain violent love of good works" (p. 40, Ayre ed.). It is no more possible for the believer to lack good works than for a fire to lack light. This is a point that matters a good deal to Benedetto. When he speaks of faith, he is not speaking of an intellectual assent to a list of propositions. He does not have in mind a dull and lifeless profession of belief, but he speaks of a transforming power. When anyone believes, God is at work. The believer commits himself to Christ in such a way that the divine power flows into him, and it is inconceivable that he remain the same. He becomes a different person, a loving person, active in the service of God and man.

Benedetto brings forth an array of scriptural passages to show the importance of faith, and then goes on to show that this has been the traditional teaching of the church by citing a string of passages from the Fathers who emphasize the significance of believing: Augustine, Origen, Basil, Hilary, Ambrose, and Bernard. He borrows from Ambrose another illustration, that of Jacob and Esau. Jacob clothed himself in Esau's robe in order to get himself the blessing of his aged father. So must we clothe ourselves "with the righteousness of Jesus Christ by faith" (p. 50, Ayre ed.).

All this does not mean that we bring in a "salvation by works" theology through the back door. We must distinguish between the works the natural man does and those that are the result of saving faith. The works that "proceed out of an unclean and foul heart are also unclean and filthy" (p. 53, Ayre ed.). The sinner does not become acceptable to God because of his works; he must first have his heart cleansed and this "proceeds of faith" (Acts 15:9, a text Benedetto quotes more than once). Only works that proceed from faith are acceptable with God. The author sees election as important; it shows us the mercy of God. But it does not work independently of faith. Unweariedly our author comes back to the necessity of saving faith.

But saving faith must be understood carefully in all its distinctiveness. Benedetto points out that faith in Christ is different from the faith that enables us to give credence to the story of Caesar or Alexander. That kind of faith is based on what men say and write; it is but human imagination and does not renew the heart nor produce good works. Again he brings us back to the thought that saving faith is productive. And again and again he repeats the thought that it is not the good works that flow from saving faith that save, but only Christ, the object of that faith. Benedetto rejects the thought that we need both faith and works for salvation (p. 57, Ayre ed.). Faith grafts us into the death and resurrection of Christ, and if we are dead with Christ, what is the point of talking about something else that we must do for our salvation?

But Benedetto is equally concerned with those who do not produce good works. While he will have nothing to do with any opinion that good works play any part whatever in producing our salvation, he is quite sure that if there are not good works then a man does not have saving faith. Thus a man may not say, "What need I to weary myself in doing good works: faith is enough to send me to paradise?" (p. 61, Ayre ed.). Such a one is reminded that the devils believe and tremble (James 2:19). As he has said before, so now he says again that good works accompany saving faith as surely as light accompanies the flame of fire. The writer illustrates his point by reminding his readers of Christ's marvelous works. These were not the cause of His deity, but the result of it. Similarly good works do not make anyone a Christian, but simply show that he is one.

Benedetto devotes a whole chapter to the way the Christian is clothed with Jesus Christ. He has referred to this before, but it is important to him and he reverts to it. This is all the more interesting in that the concept is not found in the New Testament. There we are repeatedly said to be "in" Christ, but not to have been clothed in Him. Perhaps Benedetto has in mind that quite often there are references to "putting on" Christ, where the verb is one that is often used of putting on clothing. Indeed he quotes some of them. He stretches the concept a little with his idea of "example clothing" (p. 74, Ayre ed.), which is his way of emphasizing that we must follow Christ's example. Throughout this chapter there is the stress on faith that we have seen elsewhere, together with an emphasis on the good works that accompany it. There are also some striking expressions, as when the writer speaks of Christians as "being in love with Jesus Christ" (p. 75, Ayre ed.). Being clothed with Christ means bearing the cross as well as rejoicing in the benefits the Savior has won for His own.

In view of his strong emphasis on faith, it is not surprising that before he finishes, Benedetto gives attention to "Some Remedies for the Lack of Assurance" (chapter 13). Of these he finds four to be most potent: prayer, the frequent use of Holy Communion, the remembrance of our baptism, and predestination. Of these he gives most attention to Communion and predestination. The Communion is "a token and faithful pledge" of our salvation (p. 86, Ayre ed.), but we must not trust in the Communion itself, but in that to which it points. Where it is received without faith it is a "dangerous poison" (p. 87, Ayre ed.), so we must use the sacrament property. But when we receive it rightly, we may make ourselves "drunken in the love of God with so sweet and singular a liquor" (p. 93, Ayre ed.). The sacrament, with its coming together of many grains to make the bread, points to the unity that should characterize the many who partake of it.

Christians have always had trouble with predestination, and it is interesting that Benedetto finds it so significant. He does not see it as a problem but as an encouragement. It is grounded in the Word of God and is a comfort to us. It leads to love and removes the fear of death, sin, the Devil, and hell. Our author thinks of the gift of the Holy Spirit as "the earnest-penny of our inheritance" (p. 104, Ayre ed.; he is referring to Eph. 1:14). If the Holy Spirit then gives us assurance of our places in the heavenly family, why should we doubt our predestination?

But Benedetto knows that there are problems and objections. Once more he turns his attention to the humble and self-distrustful as he refers to people who think that no one should presume to say that he has the Holy Spirit. He points out that even people like this do not scruple to call God "Our Father," and he reasons that when we understand that God has promised certain things in Christ, it is no presumption to say that we have them. The writer complains a number of times of what he calls "Jewish minds"—those who see keeping of the law or finding merit of some other kind as the way of entrance into salvation. Predestination, so clear in the Bible, guards us against this.

A couple of times Benedetto deals with the objector who says that if he is reprobate, there is no point in good works because he is going to be lost in any case, and if he is predestined there is no point in them either, for he will certainly be saved (pp. 121–122, Ayre ed.). This he finds "devilish," and in any case those who reason like this are illogical in that they do not apply the same logic in other situations. Thus if they are ill they do not say that because they are predestined to live (or not live), there is no point in seeking the help of the doctor or of medicines. His conclusion is that good works cannot be separated from faith, a point he has made many times. The predestined are those who believe; their faith and their good works go together.

The passage of centuries means that there are some things Valdés and Benedetto have said which are not very relevant to our times, and, further, that in these days questions are raised to which the authors could not give attention. But such considerations mean no more than that they lived and wrote in another age, another place. What matters far more is that they have put on paper a very valuable discussion of the central truth of the Christian faith. We are still edified as we take notice of the things these sixteenth-century figures said. Look, for example, at what Benedetto said about the Atonement as compared to today. In recent times it is agreed among theologians of the Atonement that the various theories of the Atonement can be classed into three main groups: those that stress penalty, those that stress victory, and those that stress example. Benedetto has them all. He may not have seen our discussions, but he knew what the Bible says, and he fastens his attention on the great, eternal truths.

May those who read his words enter into those same truths.

—Leon Morris
Former Principal
Ridley College, Melbourne, Australia

NOTES

[1] A. H. Strong, *Systematic Theology* (Philadelphia: The Judson Press, 1907), p. 524.

PART I

THE EXPERIENCE OF
JUSTIFICATION BY FAITH

Selections from
One Hundred and Ten Considerations
and other writings by Juan de Valdés

CHAPTER 1

THE NATURE OF THE CHRISTIAN LIFE

Idesire from you only two things. One is that you may trust and believe no more what you read here than what is clearly founded upon the Scriptures and leads you forward to that perfect Christian love. For this is the mark by which Christ desires His followers should be distinguished from all other persons. ...

"And I also desire that your Christian intention may be to make Christ the peaceful possessor of your heart in such a manner that He may resolutely and without contradiction rule and regulate all your affairs."

—From the Preface to *The Christian Alphabet*

THE NATURE OF MAN (I)*

I have often tried to understand what it means when the Holy Scriptures speak of man as being created in the image and likeness of God (Gen. 1:26–27). As I struggled over this and consulted various authors, I made no progress in understanding the matter. For one authority led me to one opinion, then another would present me with some other view. It was only when I reflected on the matter myself that I began to understand it. Looking back, I feel sure that it was God who began to assist my understanding and will continue to give me what I still lack on the matter.

---

* This and the other numerals that follow indicate which of the 110 considerations from John T. Betts's text of 1865 is being discussed.

I understand that "the image and likeness of God" consists in what is part of God's eternal character, as well as His attributes of kindness, mercy, justice, faithfulness, and truth. As I understand it, God created man with these attributes. But the first man lost the image and likeness of God through disobedience. So he became mortal, and with his mortality he became malevolent, cruel, impious, faithless, and false. On reflection, I found these thoughts confirmed by what the apostle Paul says in Ephesians 4:22–24 and in Colossians 3:5–9.

Proceeding further, I began to see that this image of God was, in fact, in the person of Christ; it is He who expressed what was kind, merciful, just, faithful, and true. He also possesses immortality as seen in His resurrection.

Moreover, I understand that those who are called and drawn by God to the grace of the Gospel make Christ's righteousness their own. They are incorporated into Christ and recover in this present life the image of God as it is expressed in their soul and by eternal life. They recover also that which relates to the body. Thus we shall all, through Christ, come to be like God as Christ is. Each one shall be in his degree like Christ, with Christ as the head and we as the members.

In the future, it will be the greatest joy to see in men kindness, mercy, justice, faithfulness, truth, and the possession of eternal life. They indeed will be like Christ and like God. It is in this way that the glory of the Son of God is promoted, for it is through Him that we shall confess we have reached fulfillment in Him as our Head and as our Lord.

HOW THE SPIRITUAL MAN DIFFERS FROM THE NATURAL MAN (III)

We are sons of God so far as we submit to be ruled and governed by God. As the apostle Paul says: "They who are led by the Spirit of God, they are the sons of God" (Rom. 8:14). Hence it is certain that he who is a son of God will submit to be ruled and governed by God. On the other hand, those who are ruled and governed by human wisdom are the sons of Adam. Such neither know nor are conscious of any other control or rule than their own.…

The sons of God will employ physicians and medicines to preserve spiritual health. But they do this without placing confidence in either one or in the other, because all their confidence is placed in God. Being governed by God alone, they obey the will of God and depend solely upon His will. While the sons of God understand these truths through experience, others find the reality of them perplexing. For "the natural man discerns not the things of the Spirit of God" (1 Cor. 2:14).

This situation is like two men who wish to cross a great river. Someone who is well acquainted with the river comes up and says, "If you want to pass over, you will have to do this and that; but if you wish me to take you over, then follow me and do so fearlessly." One of the two men confides in his own natural abilities and in what he has been told and so begins to ford the waters alone. I take this man to represent the sons of Adam. But the other man entrusts himself to the man who is acquainted with the river and follows him. This man represents the sons of God.

The folly, presumption, and errors of the natural man are much greater than the illustration of the man who crosses the river without a guide. I firmly believe that it is the prudence and the discretion of the sons of God to submit to be ruled and governed by the Spirit of Christ. This is much deeper truth than the illustration of the man who went to the guide.

So it can be understood that we are the sons of God as we are incorporated into Jesus Christ our Lord.

CONDITIONS OF ENTRY INTO THE KINGDOM OF GOD (v)

Man does not naturally confide in his fellow man unless it is for something that he cannot do by himself. Neither will he trust God unless he sees that it is impossible for him to do it by himself. Such is the willfulness of the human spirit.

Therefore, the more a man is blessed with advantages, the more difficult it is for him to be brought to a position where he can confide in God. We see this illustrated in the sick. They only resign themselves to the will of God when they are destitute of all other means to pay for physicians and medicines or have given up all hope in human help. As I reflect upon this perversity, I cannot help seeing the goodness of God that He should keep His word to help those who submit themselves to Him.

What we see in such outward circumstances is even more true of things inwardly. For man never commits his justification, his resurrection, or his eternal life to God until he knows and sees that these are unattainable by any creaturely agency. Reflecting on this, I can begin to understand why Christ said in Matthew 19:23, "that it is difficult for a rich man to enter the kingdom of heaven." That is to say, such a person is forced to resign himself to the will of God and allow himself to be guided and governed by God. This can only take place when he renounces human wisdom and the assistance of creaturely things.

So I gather that God first has to open the eyes of any man, whether he be rich or poor, whom He proposes to introduce into His Kingdom. A man will only know by his own impotence how impossible it is for a creature to give God that which He purposes and desires.

Those who are in the Kingdom of God are "the poor in spirit," whom Christ commends (Matt. 5:3). This is what David felt when in Psalm 40:17 he called himself "poor and needy." Those who have partly attained will pray "Thy Kingdom come." In the light of this, I understand why John began his preaching with the announcement of the Kingdom. This, too, is the reason Christ began to declare the advent of the Kingdom, and why He sent the apostles to proclaim it also. This is both the beginning and the end of Christian preaching, to constrain men to enter into the Kingdom by renouncing their confidence in the kingdom of this world and all that belongs to it.

Those who belong to the Kingdom of God have the Spirit declaring and recognizing everything as proceeding from the favor of God through Jesus Christ our Lord.

GOOD RESOLUTIONS ARE NOT ENOUGH (VII)

It has been my experience that the many pious, holy, and Christian things I want to do have never been fulfilled. Yet there have been many such things that I have succeeded in doing without ever really being aware that I was doing them. So this has perplexed me. It did not worry me that I often resolved to do things which I never fulfilled. But I did wonder why the same thing should occur to me with reference to things about my Christian life.

Being perplexed, I read the declaration of the apostle Peter in Mark 14:31: "If I should die for Thee, I will not deny Thee in any wise." I saw that while his resolution was pious, holy, and Christian, the issue was the reverse of what he had resolved. Then I began to realize that my resolution did not take into account my inability to carry it into effect. On the other hand, I saw that He fulfilled my desires when I never attempted to do them on my own.

From this I began to realize that I must depend upon His will. I must never resolve or propose to do anything without having Him present in my mind. I must lay before Him my desires and trust that He will bring them to pass.

From this I began to realize how futile it was to say "I will do thus and thus," because I knew my inability to carry my resolutions out. Instead of daring to make resolutions, I began to desire to be ever conformed to the will of God and to leave the execution of it with God. Thus I began to desire to be ruled by love, hope, and self-heightened denial. That is to say, I began all that was conducive to make me like Christ and like God and in all things to be a blessing to my neighbors.

So I urge every Christian to thus regulate himself or, more properly speaking, to submit himself to be ruled by God. For I assure him that God will not only fulfill his desires, but He will satisfy him in many other ways to the glory of God, to his own edification, and to the blessing of his neighbors. Without his ever thinking of them, hoping for them, or desiring to do them himself, he will do them. For God will do all this through Jesus Christ our Lord.

GOD'S COVENANT IN JESUS CHRIST (viii)

Since we owe our very existence to God, we were created with the obligation to love God, to depend upon Him, and to submit to His rule. Yet another law rules in our being, that of disobedience (Rom. 3:20). And so powerful is this law of sin that, try as we may, we never succeed in pleasing God as we should. In knowing this, God sent His Son to fill our obligation on our behalf.

In believing in the righteousness of Christ, we are saved from the penalty of disobedience. We have failed to obey our covenant of creation. So instead we have been justified and adopted into God's family to have eternal life.

Human wisdom is incapable of recognizing the reality of this covenant. In the first place, it looks at Christ as only an ordinary man; so it does not realize that He is the Son of God. Knowing this requires the gifts of God's revelation.

In the second place, we also need the revelation of Christ as risen and glorified. Having this faith, we too shall rise again as Christ has risen and as God accomplished in us what He did in Christ. Human wisdom finds no evidence to believe in the Resurrection, and so it does not believe in it.

The third aspect of the new covenant is that we believe that Christ lives glorified ever before God. It is this faith that gives us eternal life. But again, human wisdom finds no grounds to believe in an afterlife.

Thus we accept four realities in this covenant in Christ. First, we believe in Christ for salvation and are free from the punishment that is so justly due to us. Second, we believe in Christ for justification so that we are assured of our fellowship in His divine nature. Third, we believe in Christ's resurrection, and so we have eternal life in His risen life. Fourth, we believe in being His children, and so we are freed from the natural inclination to sin.

In believing these four realities, we see how God works them in us. We enjoy the first two in this life, and we shall enjoy the latter two in a future life. In the meanwhile, let us wait and persevere in the covenant that has been made for us by Jesus Christ our Lord.

CHRISTIAN LIFE CONSISTS IN BEING DEAD TO THE WORLD AND ALIVE TO GOD (xix)

The name "Christian" was first viewed in the eyes of the world as something to be despised; it was dishonorable and abject. Thus to be a Christian meant to renounce all ambition, status, and success, and to judge one's self dead to the world. That is why it was after the sacrament of baptism that they could call themselves "Christians." Thus they knew that they were God's elect and therefore were called to holiness. Only then could they call themselves by the name "Christian," for Christ had died for them and now they died in Christ. They were buried with Christ in baptism. So it is that Christ now lives, "we being dead and buried … should walk in newness of life" (Rom. 6:4).

However, it was when the name "Christian" became honorable and prestigious in the eyes of the world that kings and emperors began to feel honored to apply it to themselves. It was then that baptism began to be granted, to those who were not dead to the world. Hence the words of the apostle Paul have no reference to them, for they were neither dead with Christ nor had they risen with Christ; for they cannot be raised from the dead who have never died.

From this we see that we cannot call ourselves "Christians" until we too have been buried in baptism with Christ. For it is in His death that resurrection begins, and where I begin to live "in Christ." Once we have this purpose and resolution, then we must live watchful, disciplined lives.

So whenever we recognize any affection or appetite that belongs to a man who is alive to the world, we must quickly slay it because "this is not mine, nor does it belong to me, for I am dead to the world." Again I argue, "If I am not alive to the world," why then should I esteem or desire those things that are not honored and prized by God? Instead I should aim and desire those things that are of God. And the divine things which the Christian ought to aim at and strive after are of the Holy Spirit. For He alone is able to engage in those desires with Jesus Christ our Lord.

THE QUICKENING OF THE SPIRITUAL LIFE IS DYING TO THE WORLD (xxxix)

It is certain that as soon as a man is inspired by God to accept the covenant of justification through Jesus Christ our Lord, then he begins to die to the world and to live for God. He has to die to Adam if he is to live to Christ. He has to withdraw from the kingdom of this world if he is to enter into the Kingdom of God. When a man dies and the soul separates itself from the body, he consummates the dying to the world to Adam and to the kingdom of the world. Then he will rise again and be reunited holy to God and living to Christ.

But I realize that there is a major difference between these: the condition of a man who is quickened toward God and Christ while he is still alive in this world and the condition in which he will be when raised again to God and Christ in eternal life. It is the difference between the state of resurrection and that of spiritual renewal I discuss here.

There is indeed therefore a much greater difference between a man raised from the dead and one that is only quickened. In a comparative way, there is a difference between a man who is dead and one who is mortified. For the man who is mortified lives as if he were dead, being crucified to the world and to himself. But he still remains subject to his earthly passions and to the final reality of death. But in resurrection, he will be freed from all these things. Realizing this, I am accustomed to describe mortification therefore

44

as incomplete death and consider quickening as incomplete resurrection. But I understand that the resurrection in the life eternal will go beyond the quickening in this life. I mean to say that the glory of the resurrection will respond to the perfection of the quickening.

I understand that since quickening in this life has fixed relations with mortification, and the glory of the resurrection in life eternal will have fixed relations with the quickening, it is the duty of the devout Christian who desires to realize life eternal to mortify himself greatly. He needs to be more like Christ in his death in order that he may likewise be more like Christ in the resurrection. For in this he will remain forever in the Kingdom of God, together with God's own Son, Jesus Christ our Lord.

CHAPTER 2

KNOWING GOD

As you experience and enjoy the sweetness of the love of Christ here in this world, see this as an earnest of what is yet to come when you will be perpetually with Him. Then you will not hesitate to call it Eternal Life. And when you enjoy this as an inward experience, yours will be truly a living faith. Because you have the *experience of it actually within yourself.*

"So note well, Signora, and consider the fruit you will gather from the Kingdom of God through Christ living in your soul. Then I am sure you will willingly forget much of yourself in order to enter into this divine acquaintance. Indeed, you ought to enter into it many times each day if you wish to walk the Christian path."

—From a letter to Guilia

THE KNOWLEDGE OF GOOD AND EVIL (CVI)

According to what I read of the Creation and the fall of man, I realize that man was first created in the image and likeness of God. He was placed in the garden called the earthly paradise. But after he ate of the Tree of the Knowledge of Good and Evil, he lost the image of the likeness of God. He was expelled from the earthly paradise and now retains the knowledge of both good and evil.

I understand that it is unnatural to man and foreign to his first creation to remain excluded from the earthly paradise. Likewise it is unnatural for him to possess "the knowledge of good and evil." By what I experience in man's restoration, in his regeneration, and in his being made a new creature, I realize that he does recover the image and likeness of God. For in accepting the grace of the Gospel, he receives the remission of sins and reconciliation with God;

through the execution of the justice of God upon Christ, he thus enters into the Kingdom of God.

Under the guidance of the Holy Spirit, man subdues his intellect to renounce and mortify his human wisdom and his natural ability. What the Holy Scriptures call the knowledge of good and evil, the worldly wise call "the light of nature, of wisdom, and of human reason." And so I understand that man is constrained to subdue his intellect, mortify his wisdom and his natural light (or renounce the knowledge of good and evil), and thus obtain restoration, regeneration, and Christian renewal. For it is most just that man regain what he lost if he should first renounce what he has gained. If he has to regain spiritual life, let him renounce natural light.

If it is true that what we gain from the world is foreign to the mode of being that we now have, then we must rid ourselves of what is not natural to the being we receive primarily at creation. Regeneration and Christian renewal consist of this. To accept the Gospel and be incorporated into Christ is to gradually advance in the recovery of that mode of being. It is to recover that position and dignity of which the first man was created. But this also means that we progressively get rid of that mode, position, and dignity into which the first man has remained after he fell.

The natural light that we now have does not date from our first creation. But the first man did not recognize spiritual light to be a thing peculiarly his own and communicated by the favor of God. Desiring the knowledge of good and evil, he pretended that it would be natural to him, as indeed it has been since the Fall.

A man will require more or less of this knowledge of good and evil as he is more or less purged and purified from the affections and appetites of the flesh. Hence I think that the worldly wise among men have been led to believe that the knowledge of good and evil is a spiritual thing; they think it originates from the first creation of man. But the knowledge of good and evil and the light of nature constitute the nature of fallen man. Spiritual light had constituted man's nature in the first state of creation and now does so in his state of restoration.

Two things contradict the belief that the knowledge of good and evil is a spiritual trait. The first is what the apostle Paul says in Romans 1:19–20. The Gentiles might have been able to know God by the light of nature. The same apostle states in Romans 2:14–15 that they ought by nature to have known the will of God. Yet it appears that the light of nature does not date from the fall of man but from the period of his first creation.

The second is that the saints of old, for example David or the apostle Paul himself, availed themselves in their writings of the light of nature, wisdom, and human reason. So these things appear neither to be bad, nor to be renounced; neither to be got rid of, nor to be mortified.

In reply to the first, I understand that the apostle Paul desired to convict the Gentiles. For they excused themselves by saying that they had not been able to know God. Thus they had not adored Him, nor had they been able to know the will of God. For that reason they had lived unrighteously.

God demonstrates to them that although they did not have the knowledge of God so that they could adore Him, nor had they the will of God so that they could obey Him since such knowledge is derived from spiritual light, nor had they the knowledge which the Jews had through their Holy Scriptures, they were still at fault. So they had no excuse whatever. It is not to be inferred, then, from the apostle Paul's statement that the Christian has to totally renounce his natural reason. For the light of nature suffices to know God after a certain fashion and also to understand the will of God.

As for the second objection, it may be affirmed that the saints avail themselves in their writings of reason to the extent of its powers. Yet through spiritual light they have renounced it and mortified it because of its impotence. Instead, being justified through Christ and reconciled with God, they live under the rule and sway of the Holy Spirit in all things heavenly, spiritual, and divine.

I can well understand that the happiness and perfection of man would be so much greater if the knowledge of good and evil was wholly done away with. And in its place, the spiritual light could burn wholly and alive. But I also understand that mortal flesh is not capable of such blessing. It will become so after the Resurrection when it will have attained immortality and be unchanging. In the meanwhile, saints need to avail themselves of the knowledge of good and evil and the light of nature in order to converse in relationships with men who avail themselves of the same knowledge and of the same light. And so they follow Christ's advice in Matthew 10:16: "Be as wise as serpents." Likewise the apostle Paul admonished us in 1 Corinthians 14:20, "But in understanding be men."

Two things now occur to me.

The first is that the knowledge of good and evil, the light of nature, wisdom, and human reason have come into human possession by disobedience to God. They are connected with man's fallen estate. So it follows that this knowledge, light, and wisdom never yield real happiness to man. For as Solomon declares in Ecclesiastes 1:18, in the increase of knowledge, light, and wisdom is the increase of affliction, sorrow, and grief, and thus happiness is diminished.

The second thing is that Adam prior to his knowledge of good and evil was not ashamed to be naked. But after this knowledge he was. So I begin to realize that as long as man has spiritual life and avails himself of it, he will recognize no defect in the works of God. He will not try to correct and change them. But as long as he has the knowledge of good and evil and avails himself of this, he will try to discover defects in the works of God and pretend to correct and amend them.

Such then is the arrogance of men who glory in the possession of good and evil. In possessing great natural light, great wisdom, and great human reason this will be what we do. Conversely, humility is the possession of those who have spiritual light and take their place in the Kingdom of God. They are upheld by the faith of the Gospel, because they are incorporated into the Son of God, Jesus Christ our Lord.

MAN'S BLESSING CONSISTS OF KNOWING GOD (II)

Many have tried to find out in what man's intrinsic happiness lies. But in doing so by human reason, they have all erred in their imaginations and their knowledge has been misleading. What then do the words of the Lord mean? "This is life eternal, to know thee, the only true God, and Jesus Christ whom thou hast sent" (John 17:3). Only those who cease to be as natural man can learn what it means to put on "the image of Christ." Because they alone who are in Christ know Christ; and through Christ they can know God.

Indeed, man may attain to a certain knowledge of God by the contemplation of His creation. But they do not achieve full blessing by this knowledge. True blessing is not to be found in this kind of knowledge which they may have acquired by themselves. For it alone is found in those who have ceased to be merely themselves and instead have become united into Christ.

Trying to know God through His creation is like an inferior artist who looks at the paintings of a much more skilled painter. Such knowledge is still second-hand. But assume he was to have present within him the very spirit and genius of the famous artist himself. How different would be the skill of his perception. So it is with those who know Christ and are incorporated into Christ. They have a knowledge of God which is the knowledge that comes only through Jesus Christ. Those who know God in this way will know Him in a much deeper way when they read the Scriptures.

Having learned this, I now can understand what man's true happiness consists of; and it makes me very blessed. For now I understand much better the great obligation men have to God who depend upon Him and the Son of God, Jesus Christ our Lord.

FOUR WAYS OF KNOWING GOD
IN CHRIST (LXXXV)

I have spoken frequently of the knowledge of God as the most important reality of life, since it involves blessing and eternal life.

I find also that there are three ways to know God. The first way is by the contemplation of creation; this is also available to the Devil. The second is by the perusal of the Holy Scriptures; this is available to the Jews. But the third is through Christ; this is what is distinctive to Christians.

But having said the above, I find also that there are four ways by which we, as Christians, know God through Christ. The first is by the revelation of Christ. The second is by the communication of the Holy Spirit. The third is by regeneration and Christian renewal. The fourth is by having a certain inward vision.

I understand that the Christian knows God by the revelation of Christ when Christ permits Himself to be known to him. When in Him, we know God because He is the express image of God. "Philip, he who sees Me sees the Father also" (John 14:9). It is also what the apostle Paul says, speaking of Christ: "Who is the image of the invisible God" (Col. 1:15). And it is certain that the Christian knows God by the revelation of Christ by yet another passage: "Neither knoweth any man the Father, save the Son. And he to whomsoever the Son will reveal Him" (Matt. 11:27).

I understand that this revelation is inward and not external, and that it presupposes the knowledge of Christ. This knowledge consists in the reality of Christ's deity, His humanity, His divine and human existence, His glory and shame, His dignity and lowliness, and all else that proceeds from the revelation of Christ. It is also certain that I know Christ to be the image of God and see power, justice, truth, and faithfulness in Him.

Second, I understand that the Christian knows God by the communication of the Holy Spirit, because I understand that the Holy Spirit is given to a person in order to believe in Christ. As the apostle Paul says: "The Spirit searches all the deep things of God" (1 Cor. 2:10).

I also understand that we know God Himself, and, through Christ, the Holy Spirit is given to us by Christ Himself. It is He who enables us to know the wisdom that is in God through the wisdom acquired by the Holy Spirit. It is He who helps me to know the justice in God, for He justifies me in Christ. He helps me to know the truth in God, as He fulfills in me what He has promised. He helps me to know the goodness and mercy in God, because He bears with my infirmities and sins. Thus I am brought to recognize all these things in God, not only in relation to Scripture, but by the experience which is given me by the Holy Spirit.

Third, I understand that the Christian knows God by regeneration and renewal. For I understand that he who has been regenerated and renewed by the Holy Spirit will seek to rid himself of the image of Adam and recover the image of God in grace. We thus become the children of grace, the adopted sons of God. We become the friends of God, in piety, obedience, and faithfulness. By degrees we come to recognize the reality of God within us.

Fourth, I understand that the Christian knows God by a certain inward vision. This comes after he has known Him by the revelation of Christ, by the communication of the Holy Spirit, and by Christian regeneration. Seized with such a desire for this knowledge, he will continually follow after God pleading: "Show me Thy face" (Exod. 33:18). I am also sure that God will show Himself to such as requested. Yet we also know that this will only finally be reserved for us in the life eternal. There, seeing God perpetually, face-to-face, we shall experience the highest bliss with Jesus Christ our Lord.

BELIEVING WITH DIFFICULTY IS BETTER THAN TO DO SO WITH EASE (x)

Among those who bear the name of Christian, I know that there are two classes of men. One finds it extremely easy to believe all that is said to them in matters of religion. For the other it is extremely difficult. It appears to me that the facility of belief in the first group comes from superstition and superficial thought, while the difficulty in the other comes from excessive reflection. The one never exercises prudence, while the other finds it hard to believe anything at all. So the one will believe many things that are false, perhaps giving more credit to the false than to the true. While the other never believes in the false, but also hesitates to ever accept the truth.

Pondering on this matter, I find that only the Holy Spirit can help both classes of men. On the one hand, the Spirit of God will gradually disabuse the former of what is false, while He will authenticate to the other the things that are true. Both struggle, one to be more critical, the other to be less cynical.

While both of them struggle, I believe that they who find it hard to believe anything are in a better position to receive God's Spirit. First, this is because it is easier to recognize the truth than falsehood. Second, whoever believes readily is the more easily deceived. Third, he who easily believes may also live much longer under delusions, such as those in the early church who were converted from Judaism. I am also convinced that he who believes without being taught by the Spirit of God will rely more upon human opinion than upon a personal faith.

However, Christian faith is not based upon hearsay, but upon divine revelation alone. It is this that blesses us and brings us new hope and love. It is this that purifies the heart, and it is this that in every way pleases God. May we then be enriched with this by God Himself through Jesus Christ our Lord!

THE MERIT OF CHRISTIAN DOUBT (CIII)

I want to return to what I have frequently mentioned; namely, that a man who is tempted to doubt experiences a work of Christian progress. I believe that such temptation originates in a man's desire to believe and to stand firm in his Christian faith. The ungodly are not tempted to doubt, because they neither wish nor desire to believe. Nor are even the superstitious tempted to doubt, because as they believe in human natural wisdom, they have nobody to tempt them to doubt. Those who have made progress in the Christian life are little tempted to doubt. Having been confirmed in their faith by much experience, they have learned to disarm their enemies.

I am speaking of those who are incapable of possessing as much faith as they need, and so are not wholly free from the temptation to doubt. For God gives them faith according to their capacity. They have renounced unbelief, and they have begun by the help of the Holy Spirit to accept the pardon which the Gospel announces and to bear truth in Christian life. But they still find that human wisdom is active in them; evil spirits avail themselves of this wisdom in order to tempt them to doubt.

Such are those who have renounced self-heightened justification and have embraced the righteousness of Christ that the Gospel offers. But at the same time, they do not yet see clearly all the resources that Christ offers. When such a person begins to doubt, let him counteract such a temptation in the following ways.

In the first place, let one who doubts regard this temptation as evidence of his progress in the Christian life. Let him recognize that had he not wished a desire to believe, he would not be so tempted to doubt. His very distress is indicative of the presence of the Holy Spirit in his life.

In the second place, let him argue like this: If this Christian faith that I have were not something spiritual and divine, it would not find in me the contradiction that it does find. Let this comfort me.

In the third place, let him also argue like this: If this Christian faith were not the gift of God, I would not feel such inward new desires to please God, to be united always to Him, and to see Him glorified and sanctified by all men. These are the desires I now feel since I have surrendered myself totally to the faith. So let this, with the experience of the love of God, assure him of the truth that the Gospel affirms.

In the fourth place, let him also think like this: If a Christian's faith was not spiritual and divine, it would not give rise to that abhorrence of earthly things that I no longer pursue or desire as I used to.

Finally, let him think like this: If I knew of any alternative that is better than this, or even equal to this, in getting me to appear before the judgment of God, I might have good cause to doubt the truth to which I now cling. But since I see no alternative that is better or equal to it, I have no cause to doubt.

And so in this way, let him be assured that he is on the side to win and not to lose; by persevering in this Christian faith he cannot lose but win. Let him realize that he knows himself to be pardoned through Christ and reconciled to God through Christ. Since he realizes himself to be dead with Christ, raised again with Christ, and expecting his fulfillment with Christ, let these things assure him.

The Christian who desires to accept the righteousness of Christ will be disturbed with suggestions that tempt him to doubt. But let him take a stand here and close the door to those who threaten to assail him. Let him commend himself to God, saying with Hezekiah, "O Lord, I am oppressed; undertake for me" (Isa. 38:14). Let him be sure that God will help him and fulfill what He promised to David, "I will be with him in trouble; I will deliver him and honor him" (Ps. 91:15).

CHRISTIAN UNDERSTANDING
DEPENDS UPON GOD (xviii)

Jesus Christ says that no man comes to Him unless His Father draws him (John 6:44). The apostle Paul says also, "All have not faith" (2 Thess. 3:2) and "faith is the gift of God" (Eph. 2:8). From this I understand that it is not a man's power to believe, to love, and to confide. Nor is it in the power of man to know God or to know himself. All of this is only brought about by the distinct favor of God. For it is beyond a man's power to make himself inwardly pious, just, and holy, since it is only God that is able to effect all of this.

At the same time, it is also clear from numerous passages of Scripture that men are taught and exhorted to be devout, just, and holy. So I understand that it is every man's duty to aspire after these virtues. But if we ask for them from God, then we must seek them wholly from Him and through Him alone. Thus a Christian will withdraw his attention from any other source that will gratify or excite or distract him from the reality which is God.

But beyond everything else, the Christian should especially be concerned not to please men of the world nor to imitate their life. Let them ever remember what the apostle Paul says, "For if I yet pleased men, I should not be the servant of Christ" (Gal. 1:10).

A man can readily accomplish this by having a prayerful dependence upon God and by emphasizing the knowledge that he is living among the worst of enemies. Against these he must ever be on guard. While engaged in such spiritual exercises, it will never occur to him that through them he will acquire piety, righteousness, and holiness. Rather he will recognize that it is God alone who can give him these virtues. Just as it is the rain that blesses a soil when it has been plowed and cleared of briars and stones, so he realizes that the Holy Spirit can work on him as his mind is cleared and his bodily appetites are cleansed. For as the sun and rain are more effective upon land that has been so plowed and cleared of briars and stones, so the Holy Spirit operates more effectively upon a mind that is freed and purged from such affections and lust.

A Christian who recognizes these obligations and expects and longs for them from God will find himself much conformed to the image of God and to that of Jesus Christ our Lord within a short time.

KNOWING GOD FALSELY AND TRULY (xxxvii)

It is always true that men will follow opinions about those things of which they are ignorant; they base the opinions upon hearsay information given them by others. So when we hear that a man will lavish all his affections on what he sees, we will assume that he is vain. When we hear that he is fond of receiving money and gifts, we will presume that he is a materialist. If we hear that he is unforgiving when offended, we will regard him as inhuman and vindictive.

So when it happens that we need the services of such a person, then we will try to gain his goodwill by those things that correspond to the conceptions of him formed from gossip. However, when we continue to get to know him on terms of intimacy, we will gradually dispel these notions and relate them much more to what we have gained by personal knowledge. No longer will we strive to win his goodwill by those things that we heard from hearsay; we will approach him on things that our own knowledge has taught us.

The same thing occurs to us in reference to God. When men are deceived by human philosophy, human reason, and wisdom, then we are misled by superstition and false religion. For they represent God to us as so fastidious and irascible that we see Him as offended by everything. We will perceive Him as vindictive, the punisher of all offenses, and as so cruel that He chastises with eternal punishment. We will also see Him as so inhuman that He takes pleasure in mistreating our bodies to the extent of shedding the blood that He gave us.

In the eyes of human philosophy, we will divest ourselves of the possessions that He gave us in order that it might help us to live before Him. We will take pleasure in going naked and barefoot in continual suffering. In vain we will try to gratify Him with presents. In short, we will exercise all those things that we think delights a tyrant, because we assume that He is gratified by these things.

In fact, we are forming our notions and concepts of God merely by those representations that men have made to us about Him. The more we read and believe in this way, the more we will endeavor to behave accordingly. But when we read the Holy Scriptures, we will begin to have a very different notion of God. We will discover that a true knowledge of God is contrary to all these false conceptions about Him. Then it will come to pass that the Holy Spirit will be the true report given to us by the Holy Scriptures; by them we will conceive the true judgment and correct concept which human ignorance will never imagine.

But when men are ignorant of God and yet know they have need of Him, they will assume that He is cruel, revengeful, and insensitive to them. So they will live with constant scruples, in continual fear and terror, and with those feelings which are wont to generate hatred. Because such people conceive Him to be inhuman, they will mistreat their bodies with fasts, with vigils, with penances, and with all other things which are abhorrent to the flesh and which they assume will directly please God.

Because such hold Him to be cruel, they will sacrifice their property to Him and decorate His statue with golden ornaments and jewels. Because they hold Him to be a tyrant, they will behave themselves in the ways that one would behave before a tyrant. Such men will continue to have these attitudes before God as long as they depend upon the false notions of men.

But those who accept the Gospel are made sons of God by the covenant of justification that has been established by Jesus Christ our Lord. They now enjoy an intimate relationship with God. They know God personally, and they have a whole new perception of Him. This is not given to them by hearsay, but by personal knowledge and experience. They possess this when they have recourse in the Holy Scriptures to what they will know personally by experience. They will then understand that God is patient, merciful, slow to anger, and indeed a stranger to vengeance, except to those who are the vessels of wrath.

Understanding this, they will banish from their minds all their former scruples, fears, and terrors. For they now understand that God is so kind as to give men eternal life by sending His only begotten Son, made man, into the world. Upon Him He has executed the rigor of His justice. From this they will know that God takes no great pleasure in men's mistreatment of their own bodies. Rather He desires that they should be so divested of self-love that He is pleased neither by their asceticism nor by their dispossession of material things. Instead they will see that they are willing to give up everything if this is God's call to them. Such giving up then comes in the service of the ministry and the revelation of the Gospel.

People who now have this fresh view and new conception of God will recognize God in Christ first as being just and holy. Knowing that God is pleased with righteousness and holiness, they will serve Him accordingly. Moreover, as they recognize God in all these natural things, they will surrender to Him in everything.

CHRISTIAN FAITH NEEDS THE CONFIRMATION OF EXPERIENCE (CII)

Faith is the foundation of Christianity. It consists in accepting the general pardon through divine righteousness that has already been executed upon Christ. Thus it appears to be right for a Christian to occupy himself with these considerations that are connected with faith.

Among other things that I have brought to our attention about faith is this: A man is never staunch, firm, and constant in the Christian faith until he has had some experience of what he believes. It is certain that his stability will be in exact proportion to his personal experience.

There is a parallel for us between what we believe about the Gospel and what we believe about a very learned and spiritual man. I mean to say this: Just as we believed in the wisdom and spirituality of this man by the report of others, were others to come and make us an opposite report, we would change the opinion that we held of him. We should at least entertain doubts concerning him until closer intimacy would help us to know by experience that the first report made to us was true. Then no man would be able to persuade us to the contrary.

So it is when we come to believe that the Gospel says God has punished in Christ all our sins. This is a report that has been made to us by those who preach the Gospel. But we are in danger if other preachers come to declare the opposite, to change our belief, or at least to make us doubt what we first heard preached. Then we need to experience what is preached in the Gospel in order to stand firm and constant in what we believe. Then all the men in the world will not be able to divert or alienate us from our faith since it was now established by our own experience. For this will happen to us as long as our faith is not established upon experience.

If anyone asks me how experience of faith is acquired, I reply to him that man has experience of what he believes when he has peace of conscience. Then it will seem to him that he could appear before God in judgment safely. He would then sense the same safety he would have had were he to live with all the innocence in which Christ lived and to suffer by the will of God what Christ suffered.

Moreover, I reply that mortification and quickening in the Spirit are the most effective forms of experience by which our faith is established.

But supposing someone asks me, "How shall I, a believer, confirm my faith by experience?" I would reply with two things.

First of all, let him divest himself of all Christless modes of justification, both of those that are negative as well as those that are positive. Let him only embrace the justification that is in Christ, which consists in believing. Let him strive in prayer to God and ask that He would cause him to feel peace of conscience, that He would mortify him, and that He would quicken him.

In the second place, let him keep the strictest reckoning with himself as to his works, words, and thoughts. He will know by these means what progress he has made in mortification and quickening. Let his purpose be to increase every day his experience of mortification and quickening so that he strives to acquire that Christian experience by which Christian faith is established.

What about the man who is anxious to know how he can get rid of his own self-justification? I would advise that he strip himself of both those things that are negative as well as positive. Concerning those things which are negative, let him know that if he does not kill, steal, act as a fornicator, or injure his neighbor, it is either because he is not inclined to do so or because he fears social disgrace and the penalty which attaches to these crimes during his life. Let him refrain from doing other things to which he is inclined that do not involve social disgrace and are not punished in this life, such as ambition, honor, self-pleasure, and his own reputation.

Moreover, I will tell him that he must divest himself of the things that are positive also. He should know the way in which the supernatural has blended with some of them on the one hand, and on the other hand how self-love has contaminated and defiled the rest. In this way he will deprive and strip himself of every false mode of justification. As a result let him embrace what the Gospel offers him. It will show him that God punished all our sins in His only begotten Son, Jesus Christ our Lord.

THE CHRISTIAN'S FAITH IS IN PROPORTION TO HIS KNOWLEDGE OF GOD IN CHRIST (LXIX)

As I consider the great emphasis that our Lord Jesus Christ gives to faith, I realize that He declares even a small amount of it enough to remove mountains (Matt. 17:20). Then I look to myself and find how lacking I am in the power of such faith. I find how weak and feeble my faith is. Then I direct my spirit to God and say with the apostles, "Lord, increase my faith" (Luke 17:5), and with the father of the lunatic child, "Lord, help mine unbelief" (Mark 9:24).

Realizing that faith comes to me as a gift from God, and yet realizing that I have faith in proportion to my personal knowledge of God in Christ, I address myself to God. I ask Him to even make Himself known to me, to let me see Him. I ask He will grant it to me, to know and to see Christ as much as possible in this present life. I seek this to have confidence, and that in this way my faith will become strong and effectual.

For I see that it is the guile of the human race's enemy, and arch-enemy of Christ, to seek to lead men away from faith. Satan endeavors to make those who accept the Gospel of Christ continue to be unbelieving or skeptical. Persuading themselves that their honor is involved in their belief, they do not really recognize how lacking they are in faith. They never come to realize that

Christ insists upon their seeking the knowledge of God in Christ. They never realize that such knowledge is based only upon faith. They do not see the connection of such faith with justification. Nor do they see that it is only through justification that they can receive glory and eternal life.

Such is the blindness of man who sees only through the eyes of human wisdom. But the greatest blindness of men is that they reject personal experience and accept hearsay evidence in divine matters, both for themselves and for others. They do not abide by the reality of personal experience. Even worse, they rebuke those who seek such certain knowledge in personal experience.

But I realize that only those persons who have such certain knowledge in divine things know God and Christ through revelation and inspiration. Only they can truly testify and have a real testimony.

Others, if they give secondhand evidence concerning this, do not give a true testimony. For they do not feel what they speak about.

Those persons that have experienced these things of God, those who find and feel within them the results which the knowledge of Christ works inwardly, those whom we thereby make righteous—it is those people who live in true piety and justification. The rest of mankind tries to give evidence of such matters, yet they have not the experience. And so their testimony is not true, for they do not feel what they speak about.

I gather from all this that a man ought naturally to judge himself as lacking faith and therefore as unable to move mountains. Admitting this, he ought to ask God to give him faith. He ought not to be content with hearsay and theoretical knowledge. Rather he needs that which is based upon the certainty of personal experience.

So I am forced to the conclusion that a man has as much faith as he has personal knowledge of God in Christ. It is by such faith that a man obtains justification, and by justification, glory and eternal life. For God is able to give a man in a moment of time such knowledge of Himself and of Christ as is sufficient to induce belief. So we ought never to despair of the salvation of man so long as there is breath in the body, ever hoping that God may do that which He is able and willing to do. For He lets Himself be known and shows man Christ in order that he may believe and love. In so believing, he may enjoy Christian justification and go to live and reign with Jesus Christ our Lord.

CHAPTER 3

THE HOLY SPIRIT IN THE LIFE OF THE BELIEVER

Though I speak with the tongues of men and of angels, and have not charity, I am become as sounding brass or a tinkling cymbal" (1 Cor. 13:1).

"The Apostle's purpose in saying this is to console and encourage the Corinthians who had not received those external gifts of the Holy Spirit bestowed upon many believers at that time. He does this by showing that the man who possesses charity, or Christian love, has attained greater excellence. Such a person is in a better position than someone else who possesses all the external gifts of the Holy Spirit in the highest degree possible. It is in such Christian love that the Apostle intends to set forth the more excellent way which he told the Corinthians he could show them. By 'charity' he understands the love, or affection, which the man who has accepted the grace of the Gospel cherishes toward God and Christ. He loves as well the things of God and Christ, and he loves God for Himself and the things of God for God's sake.

"I understand this love is wrought in man by the Holy Spirit, whom he receives upon belief and more abundantly as his faith grows. The measure of the Holy Spirit's influence within a man, then, is determined by the amount of faith he has. The measure of the fervor of the love within a man is determined by the amount of the Holy Spirit's influence that operates upon him. So all this excellence that the Apostle attributes to love he could equally have attributed to faith, since there is no difference between the fruit or the roots of a tree. Faith is the root, and the fruit is love."

—From *Commentary on First Corinthians*

WALKING THE CHRISTIAN WAY WITHOUT THE HOLY SPIRIT IS LIKE WALKING IN DARKNESS (xlvi)

Those who are only guided by the light of human nature and wisdom while presuming to understand the things that belong to the Spirit of God may be compared to the man who walks at night. It is a way full of perils and obstacles because one cannot see.

As he walks in the twilight, a man may think that a tree appears to be a robber and he flies from it. Or a rock looks like an armed robber and he is dismayed. Or at other moments water appears to him to be like a stone and he plunges into it. Or a shadow will appear to be like a tree, and he tries to lean against it, only to fall flat on the ground. So is the man who is merely guided by the light of nature as he seeks to tread the road to God.

At times the man who walks by human guidance will be frightened by things that ought never to have terrified him at all. At other times he will feel secure and trust the things in which he never should feel secure. Or he will distrust everything and grope, walking like one bewildered and unsure of where he is going.

There is another who walks by the light of Holy Scripture in the pattern of the saints but without having the Holy Spirit. I compare him to a man who walks at night and carries a candle in his hand so that he is not entirely in the dark. But he does not go without fear; his mind will not feel safe, nor will he feel sure that he will not fall into many difficulties.

The best advice to give the traveler who walks by night simply with the light of his own eyes is that it would be better for him to stop journeying as long as the night lasts; and he should wait until the sun has risen again to show him the way. So it is better not to travel on the road to God by the mere light of reason, by the reading of the Scripture, or by the example of the lives of the saints. For one still journeys through the night of his own blindness until God sends him His Spirit. By means of the Spirit he may thoroughly know his way and see all that is before him.

But suppose someone asks me, "How can I halt on such a road?"

My answer to him is, "Do not exercise yourself in anything effecting righteousness or in any kind of self-exerted religion. Instead, pray earnestly to God that He will send you His Spirit, that He will be to you as the sun upon the road. Then you will neither walk by your own intelligence or your mere wisdom. During the time that God delays in sending His Spirit to you, apply yourself to everything you recognize as true devotion without any mixture of superstition. Be content with all that God does, and be discontented with all that you do yourself." This is what my advice would be to him.

Just as the sun will shine once more and rise to its full splendor, so the eyes of the traveler of whom I have spoken will be like the gift of the Spirit given in a moment of time. He will see that our God, who is rich in grace and mercy, gives to us His Spirit in such measure that it will profit and not injure us. For He comes not according to our own craving, but according to His own eternal wisdom. Thus He gives as a good Father. So He governs them who are His children and who have been incorporated in His only begotten Son, Jesus Christ our Lord.

GOD'S PRESENCE IS ONLY KNOWN BY HIS HOLY SPIRIT (XXIII)

Finding my mind dried up and sterile and as if it were cut off from God, I tried to remedy this by meditating solely upon God. But no sooner had I made this decision than I began to realize that it was not in my power to meditate upon God. Nor was it in my power to think about His presence in order to escape barrenness, aridity, and alienation from God. For I realized what a vast difference there is between the state of the soul when it labors to be in the presence of God and the condition when God makes a soul conscious of His presence. For the one is only the effort of the human mind, while the other is the work of the Holy Spirit. So I concluded that the same difference exists between those two states of mind as that which exists between the flesh and the spirit.

Those who seek to cut themselves off from the world and to set their affections upon God by their own strength are like those who might leave an unattractive woman and attempt to fall in love with one who is more beautiful and excitable. They do this out of appreciation of attractiveness rather than out of appreciation for life's realities. So those who seek to know God by their own energies waste their efforts, because they are not moved to love God as He really is.

Rather, the reality is what Jesus said to the disciples: "You have not chosen Me, but I have chosen you" (John 15:16). It is as if He had said, "You did not set your affections upon Me, but I have set Mine upon you." The apostle John expressed a similar idea saying that to be a son of God, one must become so not by the will of the flesh, nor by the will of man, but by the will of God and through the Holy Spirit (John 1:13). For a man, then, to occupy himself in prayer before God so that he may be in love with God, he must receive the Holy Spirit. And the Spirit is only obtained by faith in Jesus Christ our Lord.

THE HOLY SPIRIT PROMPTS US TO LOVE GOD (XXIV)

God loves all men, but especially those who accept the redemption of His Son our Lord. Men naturally hate God, and those who hate Him especially do so from the depravity of their own invention. But when our sins are forgiven us by the cross of Christ, we then do all in our power to love Him as we never could have done before. Also, the Holy Spirit bids us to become disenchanted with ourselves and to be enamored with God. But nothing makes us more in love with Christ than suffering for His sake. Yet we will always be conscious that the love which He has for us is infinitely greater than any love the most devout can show to Him. So all we can do is accept the righteousness of God that is given by Jesus Christ our Lord.

THE HOLY SPIRIT GUIDES US IN UNDERSTANDING THE HOLY SCRIPTURES (xxxii)

I believe that scholarly men without the Holy Spirit suffer the same illusions with reference to the Holy Scriptures that unholy men do with images. It happens like this.

An ignorant man will keep a crucifix at the place where he enters his room in order to recall what Christ has suffered. Because he finds this suggestive, he will set up similar images in other parts of his house. As a result he will be always assured by looking at them and by his memory recollecting what Christ has suffered. So he really does not seek to imprint the reality of Christ crucified upon his inward being, nor will he therefore really taste or experience the benefit of Christ's passion. When he wants to solicit something from Christ, all he does is simply look at the effigy rather than at the reality of Christ's presence within him.

In the same way, a learned man without the Holy Spirit has in the Holy Scriptures everything recorded that is relevant to the life of a Christian. There he will find all that he ought to believe and what he ought to do. Every time he opens his book he can understand the one or the other. Because this appears sufficient for him, he will exhaust all his study and all his diligence in procuring many books that expound the Bible.

But in the process, he will not be concerned to have imprinted upon his spirit what he reads and studies. When he is moved to seek understanding of some divine mystery, he will turn to the Bible to attain the information without bowing in prayer that God will show him and teach him. So he makes the mistake of teaching his own mind and his own nature those things which men wrote who had the Spirit of God. No wonder he may become disillusioned with the Scriptures, because he does not have the Spirit of God within his own heart.

In contrast, the unlearned man, who does have the Holy Spirit, will form memory images such as the "alphabet of Christian piety."

But once these letters have been imprinted within his mind and he has experienced their reality, he will discard them as the alphabet is handed to other beginners. For when he has Christ in his soul and when he is inspired to ask of Christ, he will no longer need to fix his eyes upon a portrait. He will fix his eyes upon the impression that he has within his mind.

In the same way, the learned man who has the Spirit of God will employ the Holy Scriptures as an "alphabet of Christian piety." Likewise he will taste and experience it not with human judgments and skill in his own mind, but by the reality of the work of God within him. So when he desires to understand some divine mystery, he will go first of all to the Spirit of God and then compare what he has learned with what is written in those holy books. Then he will seek the Holy Spirit to be his Teacher and make use of the Scriptures as a kind of holy conversation that refreshes him.

Thus it is with the unlearned as well as the learned who are gifted with the Holy Spirit. They both find the fulfillment of the Gospel that was made by the prophet: "They shall all be taught of God" (Isa. 54:13). They are those who are given the Spirit of Jesus Christ our Lord.

THE HOLY SPIRIT IS EVIDENCED IN SPIRITUAL WARFARE (xxxv)

When a man wishes to do the will of God, he will find himself in much inward conflict. For the flesh will always resist the Spirit and contradict all that it stands for. There is an intense enmity between them both. So the man who has the Spirit of God, an affection for God, and a desire to conform to the will of God will live with great tension. For the man who has the Spirit will grieve, be very sensitive, and also be vexed by his personal troubles. We see how the saints under the Law were so affected. Indeed, we see in the New Testament how the Son of God Himself, Jesus Christ our Lord, deeply felt His troubles (John 11:35).

If, then, a person is moved by the Holy Spirit, he will encounter opposition, contradiction, and even outward persecution. He need not be surprised if he feels so weak and ineffective. His weakness of faith is in fact evidence of the great contradiction between the flesh and the Spirit. He needs therefore to be encouraged, to persevere, and to strive greatly in this fight.

But let the Holy Spirit have the victory and be the conqueror. For it is not fit that the son of the bondwoman, which is the flesh, should be heir with the son of the freewoman, which is the Spirit. The flesh should not be heir of those blessings which really belong to the Spirit (Gal. 4:30). But this is only possible for those who receive the blessings from Jesus Christ.

TRAITS OF A SPIRIT-FILLED LIFE (XLVII)

Our Lord Jesus Christ counsels us to be on our guard against false prophets. They may have the appearance of sheep, but they are really wolves (Matt. 7:15). They busy themselves about Christian ministry. They pretend to obtain the Spirit of God and become spiritual persons by their exercises and efforts; yet they remain counterfeit. To recognize such wolves I have discovered four marks by which spiritual persons may be discerned.

The first mark of a true Christian is to have great affection for spiritual things, to delight in them and follow anxiously after them. I call all those things spiritual which are expressions of the Holy Spirit, that is, inward and divine expressions. Examples are the study of the Holy Scriptures, frequent discourse upon holy topics, persevering prayer, and the continual worship in the Spirit. It is saying that there is a desire to enjoy continual satisfaction with God and with everything that is holy, just, and good, as far as the weakness of the flesh can admit.

The second trait is a personal abhorrence of all conversation and discourse about man or books in which there is no trace of the Holy Spirit.

The third trait is the approval of thoughts and experiences that are required by the Holy Spirit. This approval comes with the heart and not with the head. For while human wisdom may occasionally approve of spiritual things, it does so with understanding and not with the affections.

The fourth trait is the mortification of the mind and of the body. This modifies the spirit of curiosity which stimulates so much human wisdom. Human wisdom approves and teaches mortification. But however much it teaches and approves of it, there will never be a person who can truly benefit from it without the Spirit of Christ.

So I conclude that the true Christian will cherish spiritual things and be detached from and disenchanted with those in which the Holy Spirit has no part. To recognize the distinction between the true and false Christians, we will require them to avail themselves of the help that is given to us by our Lord Jesus Christ.

CHAPTER 4

THE CHRISTIAN'S
PRAYER LIFE

Prayer is the raising of the mind to God with desire to obtain what is asked of Him. The manner of prayer, and what we shall ask for in prayer, are such as Christ taught us in Matthew 6:5–6: 'When you pray, do not be like the hypocrites, for they love to pray in the congregations of the people, and in the comers of the streets, that they may be seen of men. Truly they have their reward. But you, when you pray, enter into your closet, and when you have shut the door, pray to your Father who is in secret. And your Father who sees in secret will reward you openly.' Christ teaches us by these words that our prayers should be private not only to avoid vainglory, but also because the mind when outwardly quiet will more easily be inwardly quiet as well.

"And Christ then immediately says, 'And when you pray—use not many words as the heathen do' (Matt. 6:7). In this He instructs us not to ask for vain and unnecessary things in prayer, but for those which seem essential for the glory of God, for the salvation of our neighbors and of ourselves, as well as for the support of our lives. Christ in another place teaches us to pray, saying, 'All things whatsoever you ask in prayer, believing, you shall receive' (Matt. 21:22).

"In order then for prayer to be proper, it should be in private, with few words, with much desire, and with true and just requests. It should be with entire confidence that God will give us what we ask of Him."

—From *The Christian Alphabet*

THE HOLY SPIRIT ENABLES US TO PRAY (XLVIII)

From Romans 8:26 we realize that the apostle Paul considered prayer to be one of the things in which we are aided and blessed by the Spirit of God, in spite of our weakness and infirmities. He says that since we do not know how to pray as we ought, the Spirit of God prays for us. From this I understand that the Holy Spirit prays for us when He impels us and moves us to pray, because it is at such a time that He prays in us Himself. And I understand that he who prays with the Spirit of God asks what is the will of God, and so obtains what he desires. He who prays with his own spirit can only ask what is his own self-will, and hence he neither knows what nor how he ought to pray.

The human mind is presumptuous, arrogant, and unwilling to admit that it neither knows what nor how it ought to pray. It says "I will ask God that His will be done, and thus I cannot go wrong." Such a one does not realize that this is not prayer at all. The fact is that whether we are willing or are unwilling to do the will of God, the human mind is forced to confess with the apostle Paul that we do not know what or how we ought to pray. That is why the Apostle urges us to earnestly pray to God to give us His Holy Spirit.

The way we can distinguish between praying with our own spirit or praying by the Holy Spirit is as follows. When the result of prayer is a feeling of contentment blended with pride and esteem for one's self, then we may be sure that we are not praying with the Holy Spirit. But when we have a deep sense of satisfaction blended with humility and self-mortification, then we are praying with the Holy Spirit. It is also true that if a man has never prayed with the Holy Spirit, he cannot make this distinction.

Cornelius prayed with the Holy Spirit before the apostle Peter went to his house. But he did not realize that he was praying with the Holy Spirit. Understanding this later through the ministry of the apostle Peter, Cornelius obtained from God even more than he had sought. It was not more than the Spirit of God had sought for him, but more than Cornelius had sought in his own mind (Acts 10). Likewise, the Spirit of God often prays in us and for us without our ever knowing that it is He who so prays, or without knowing what object is solicited by Him in prayer.

Human wisdom is ever opposed to the Spirit of God and pretends to know how things work. Human wisdom works things always to its own advantage, for its own glory, and for its own satisfaction, and not for the benefit of the neighbor or for the glory of God. So those who work with human wisdom will find satisfaction with their work, but it is mixed with arrogance and pride. They who work with the Holy Spirit will find satisfaction in their works of a very different kind, for their satisfaction is mixed with humility and mortification.

From these reflections I come to this conclusion: In order to pray as we ought, as well as to work, to understand, and to otherwise exercise ourselves with mind or body in this present life, we need the direction of the Spirit of God. So we need to confess that we do not know how to pray as we ought, and that we do not know how to perceive or understand as we ought. With this confession we shall ever ask of God His Holy Spirit, and He will give it to us through Jesus Christ our Lord.

FAITH IN PRAYER (XLI)

Jesus Christ our Lord assures every devout Christian that he will obtain from His eternal Father all that he asks believingly in prayer. I have experienced along with others that I sometimes obtain less of what I pray for when it appears to me that my confidence in prayer is the greatest. On the other hand, I obtain what I pray for when it appears to me that my confidence in prayer is least.

As I think about this paradox, I realize that God requires a man to have faith in prayer, just as He requires of him entire love. God well knows that a man cannot of himself love Him with his whole heart. He well knows that man cannot exert faith in prayer. For they are both contrary to his natural inclinations. So they both must of necessity proceed from God Himself.

But God requires of man that he may know himself, and in knowing himself, that he may humble himself. God knows he needs to cast himself on His mercy, and not pretend to be able to do anything by himself. Because He knows that the human mind is so proud, He is at times more deaf to a man's petition when it appears to the suppliant that his faith in prayer is the strongest.

God acts in this way so that man may not attribute what he obtains through prayer to his own faith. He does this also in order that man may know the difference that there is between his self-confidence and that assurance which comes only from God. He gives in this way so man may know God holds him in esteem and loves him, and He will occasionally give him what he asks for even when his faith is less in his own eyes. At other times He gives without being asked, simply upon His wish. Again, at other times, He gives man what he might desire, even without his really desiring it.

From this I understand that God wills man to strive with all his mind to give Him all his love. He desires that man may trust in Him alone, and that he will hope from Him all the belongings in the present life as well as in the future. With this effort, I understand that man gains two significant things. The first is that God overlooks the coolness of his love, the weakness of his faith, and the impatience of his hope. The other is that God Himself gradually influences his love, strengthens his faith, and animates his hope. And this He brings to fulfillment in Himself, which Jesus Christ our Lord has promised.

REFLECTIONS ON THE LORD'S PRAYER (LXXI)

In the most holy prayer we call our Lord's prayer, I find occasion for the following reflections.

First, when I call God Father, it is right that I see myself able to hope from God all that an obedient son can hope from an exceedingly good and loving Father. This I can do in spite of being a disobedient son. For God does not look upon me as I am in myself, but as I am in Christ of whom I am a member. He was the most obedient Son, and it is through this affiliation that I dare to call Him Father.

If I should call God Father through ordinary generation, this would imply that I did so with my natural being. Calling Him Father through personal regeneration does not come from my natural being, although I can see from my natural being what it means to be obedient or disobedient. But I call Him Father in the being of Christ, who was absolutely obedient. And so I understand that it is necessary to bring myself to be to God as a good and obedient son is to his father.

Second, I consider that in saying "Our Father," I presuppose that I hold all those as brethren who by regeneration have also God for their Father. And so I ought likewise to relate myself toward them as brethren.

Third, I consider that since God is where He is known, the Holy Scriptures are accustomed to present Him as being in heaven. It is there where He is known. God is in all His creatures, but it is not said that He abides in any of them. He does so only in those who know Him or those to whom He makes Himself known.

Fourth, I consider that it is peculiarly the desire of the devout Christian that God's name be sanctified. I mean to say that God should be esteemed and recognized by everyone as holy and just in all His works. But human wisdom does not find holiness or righteousness in many things that occur to men in this life. Such wisdom avoids the impiety of attributing injustice to God. But it falls into another trap by taking from God His particular providence in all things. So the Holy Spirit, knowing that holiness and justice arrange themselves on the side of God in all things, does not hesitate to attribute all things to God.

Thus He desires men to submit the judgment of their human wisdom to Him and to satisfy the name of God. He desires that they confess and realize that God does all things, and that holiness and justice pervade them all. There are some men who sanctify God in the things that they deem to be good. But they withdraw themselves from those things which they deem to be evil. There are others who sanctify God generally in all things, but do so only with their mouth and not with their heart. The desire of the devout Christian is that God be sanctified in all things. God desires also that the sanctification proceeds from the heart, because He wills to be sanctified in this manner.

Fifth, I consider that the devout Christian's distinct and constant desire consists in longing that the Kingdom of God may come quickly. The Kingdom will come when the resurrection of the just has been accomplished, when Christ delivers up the Kingdom to His eternal Father. For that will be the Kingdom of God in a special sense, since the just will be governed directly by God and see Him face-to-face. God already reigns in the just through Christ. It is in the same fashion that He gives light, but does so through the Son. In the light eternal He will reign Himself, as He Himself will then give light (Rev. 21:23).

Sixth, I consider that devout Christians flee from the will of God when they see it either associated with wrath or mediated through secondary causes. They supplicate that the will of God will be done here on earth as it is in heaven. By this they understand that what is associated with His mercy and love is mediated by God Himself.

Seventh, I consider that devoted Christians sense they eat the bread of anxiety and sorrow because of the sin of the first man. So they pray to God that He will supply them with ordinary food. Then they may without anxiety and sorrow be provided for and sustained according to their necessities. They acknowledge their maintenance is due solely to God's bounty. Beginning here to feel the remedy for the first man's sin, they therefore begin to experience the benefit of Christ.

Eighth, I consider that devout Christians always pray He would pardon those things on account of which He might most justly punish them. Not that they doubt the general pardon which they have had through the righteousness of God executed on Christ. On this point they are fully assured. But they rejoice in the recollection that they are debtors. For it is this remembrance that works humility in them before God.

I understand that the pardon they grant to their debtors they attribute to this cause. So they never put themselves under an obligation to pardon, but they pardon because God has already done this for them. I understand this from what Jesus Christ Himself adds in the Gospel, saying, "If you forgive, you will be forgiven" (Matt. 6:14).

Ninth, I consider that devout Christians know their weakness and fear temptation. For these things really lead to a violation of the Christian character. At the same time, they know their need of being trained in mortification by temptations. So they pray to God not that they might not be tempted, but rather that the temptations should not lead them to forfeit their Christian character.

Tenth, I consider that devout Christians are aware how numerous are the evils with which the righteous have to do battle. They fear they might succumb to them. They know the weakness of their own limited powers. So they return to God and entreat Him to deliver them from them all.

I understand that devout persons will persist and persevere in these petitions. They will do so not only because of the outward teachings of our Lord Jesus Christ which they find in the narrative of His life. But they do so because of the inward teachings of the Holy Spirit. For He implants these desires within their souls. He moves them to ask these things.

So those who pray while only being instructed by Christ's outward teaching and not being inspired by the inward teaching of the Holy Spirit do not pray like true living members of our Lord Jesus Christ.

CHAPTER 5

THE CHRISTIAN'S USE OF SCRIPTURE

N ot with wisdom of words, lest the cross of Christ should be made of no effect" (1 Cor. 1:17).

"Here the apostle Paul deals with another weakness of these Corinthians. It was their esteem of the world's wisdom. He goes on to deal with this weakness in these first chapters. He wants to eradicate it from the Christian life, for it was dangerous and pernicious. It is always accompanied by curiosity and self-esteem. In the Christian, these two vices are much more damaging since most often they appear in the guise of zeal and piety. The desire for knowledge and its associated disciplines, even the reading of the Holy Scriptures, injures the mind when the reader is not guarded against them.

"I understand a man reads the Holy Scriptures with curiosity when he does so solely with the view of acquiring knowledge. And I understand that a man reads the Holy Scriptures with self-esteem when he uses his knowledge to talk about and to criticize them.

"Someone may therefore ask me, 'Why should I read the Holy Scriptures? What is my motive?' I reply that it is for formal edification. We read them in times of hardship and suffering in order to be comforted. We read them at other times to be awakened in mind and to have fresh desires for God. We read them to conceive fresh insights of spiritual and divine realities. Or again, we do so to express the testimony of what God is doing inwardly within my soul.

"This is one of the great advantages of reading the Holy Scriptures: The man doing so discovers the extent to which his feelings and experience concur with those who possess the Holy Spirit.

Hence the person is confirmed in his conviction of the work of the Holy Spirit in his life."

—From *Commentary on First Corinthians*

THE HOLY SCRIPTURES SHOULD BE READ WITHOUT IDLE CURIOSITY (LV)

The human mind sustains itself and preserves its vigor with a mixed diet of ideas and thoughts. Yet nothing so stimulates or proves satisfactory to the mind as the habit of curiosity. This is usually associated with ambition and vanity. I believe that such curiosity is so palatable to the human mind that it will feed upon it in whatever way it is dished up.

But it is essential that this natural mind must die in those who make Christian godliness their aim. In such a way they may know what it is to die with Christ. For this to happen, the food of curiosity must be taken from them; nor must they indulge in it in any way. Setting it aside, they must especially do those things which pertain to faith and godliness. For these are the most prized for the Christian mind.

I believe the study of the Holy Scriptures for motives of curiosity is highly dangerous. While Scripture study is normally an effective weapon for slaying the human mind, the mind will convert Scripture into an idle curiosity, and will gladly feed upon this for its own sake. So I believe it is a godly Christian duty to be very vigilant and careful in the use of curiosity, especially in the study of the Holy Scriptures. The simplicity of the Spirit can be taken away and replaced by carnal curiosity. This is what happens to those who read the Holy Scriptures merely to know and understand for their own sake.

In reading the Holy Scriptures, the godly Christian should only fix his attention upon the inward realities and feelings which God by His Holy Spirit should work in his soul. By their help, he shall proceed to test the things of the Holy Spirit as he finds them in the Holy

Scriptures in order to understand his own dark background.

Therefore, do not let him assume that he understands what he has not experienced. Then he will desire to experience at least theoretically what he has understood. Let him focus his attention on his own experience. In doing this he will divest himself of idle curiosity and will seek to mortify his own mind so that he will acquire a true understanding of the Holy Scriptures. He will then realize that the occupation of a Christian does not consist merely in an accumulation of knowledge but in a lived experience of it.

He will then discern the errors into which others fall who think that they do not understand the Holy Scriptures because they have not been ordained to the priesthood, or schooled with scientific knowledge and human learning. Let them rather realize that those who have been ordained and professionally trained in fact need to renounce all of these things and leave them behind. It is then that they might acquire the true apprehension of the Holy Scriptures. These things are not acquired by knowledge or attained merely by curiosity. They can only be acquired by experience, and this is to be sought with simplicity. For God reveals His secrets to those who are trained in, and adorned with, this simplicity. Such is affirmed by God's own Son, Jesus Christ our Lord (Matt. 11:28–30).

HOW THE HOLY SCRIPTURES ARE INSPIRED BY THE HOLY SPIRIT (LXIII)

The apostle Peter in his second epistle (1:19) judges that the man who seeks to be godly will have no other light than that of the Holy Scriptures. Having no other light than that of a candle, he will be like a man standing in a dark place. Peter says that the man who seeks to be godly and has the Spirit of God to guide him, develop him, and mature him is like a man who stands on a spot where the rays of sun focus. Such a place is bright and resplendent.

Thinking about this, I have been meditating on seven things. The first is that just as the person who stands in the dark is better off with a candle than without it, so the one who seeks to be godly is better off with some light than none. He is in a dark place when he realizes his reason and human wisdom prejudice him with reference to his desire for godliness. They really do not prove much help to him and give him no light. But he realizes he is better off with the Holy Scriptures than without them.

The second condition I realize is that just as a person in a dark place does not see things as clearly and plainly with a candle as he would in the sunshine, so is the man who is intent on godliness. For he neither understands nor knows the things of God as clearly and plainly by the Holy Scriptures as he could if he were able to see and know them by the Spirit of God.

The third condition I realize is that just as a person may stand in a dark place with the light of a candle alone, he will fear the threat of being left alone in the dark should anything happen to extinguish his candle. So is the person who is intent on godliness. Having no other light than the Holy Scriptures, he is fearful of being left without light, should anything happen to deprive him of the Holy Scriptures or of the right understanding of them.

The fourth condition is like the man who stands in a dark place with the light of a candle and begins to wish he had more light. He may even snuff out the candle or get someone else to extinguish it for him. But in the process, he is left without any light at all. Such is the person who is intent on godliness but who begins to neglect the Holy Scriptures and to forget the importance of their application. So he begins to either interpret them for himself or to get someone else to interpret them for him. Eventually he may convert the Holy Scriptures into a mere human composition. Then he will remain in darkness and be so deceived that he does not realize what he has done.

The fifth condition that I have thought about is what happens when the rays of the sun penetrate into the dark place where the man had only the use of a candle. He will see much more clearly all the things that are there. The candle will become dim and lose all its original brilliance. Such is the person who desires to have the Holy Spirit enter into his mind as he desires godliness.

With the light of the Spirit he can avail himself of the Holy Scriptures. In this way he will begin to understand and know the things of God himself more clearly than he ever did before. Now he will begin to know God and to pay more attention to Him. He does so because these things are now brought to his mind by the Holy Spirit. They are not just simply the text of Scripture.

One can understand then why the apostle Peter commands the study of the Holy Scriptures and yet recognizes that they are given to a man shut up in the dark place of human wisdom and natural reason. He desires that this study will at the same time be brought under the illumination of the Holy Spirit and thus shined within the soul. He realizes that when this light comes, such a one will no longer need to seek merely the text of the Holy Scripture. For he will see the light of the coming of Christ, just as Moses saw the law in the light of the presence of the Gospel (2 Cor. 3:13–18).

The sixth condition which I have thought about is like the person who enjoys the sunshine; he knows it will never fail him. At the same time he realizes that it would be foolish to throw the candle away. It may assist others in the way it has helped him. So is the man who enjoys the light of the Holy Spirit; he is assured that He will never fail him. But he never casts aside the Holy Scriptures, for he realizes that they will continue to serve others as they have blessed him.

The seventh condition that I have thought about is that when the sunshine enters the room, it is not necessary to then examine the whole nature of the candle's composition. Likewise, the man whose mind is filled with the Holy Spirit and has availed himself of the Holy Scriptures will not seek to discover all the secrets that are involved in the making of the Scriptures. For he acts as one who has discovered the reality of the gift of the Holy Spirit.

The gifts of the Holy Spirit are varied. Likewise, the Holy Scriptures have been written by many different people who had different gifts of the Holy Spirit. Therefore they wrote differently from each other. But the Scriptures are understood by those who have the Holy Spirit, even though there is such a diversity of material. And diverse are the gifts which God communicates to them by the Holy Spirit through Jesus Christ our Lord.

PATIENCE AND COMFORT OF THE SCRIPTURES (xxxiii)

According to the apostle Paul (Rom. 15:4), those of us who are in the Kingdom of God in this life keep ourselves in the hope of eternal life by the patience and comfort of the Holy Scriptures. "Patience" means that although the fulfillment of what we desire appears to be tardy in coming, we reinforce our minds more and more and so never lose confidence. The "comfort of the Scriptures" means that reading the promises of God constantly confirms and strengthens us in hope.

Our situation is like that of a man whom the nobleman promised by letter to employ for one thousand ducats a year. The man cherished the hope of receiving that income. So patiently he strengthened his heart. As the fulfillment of the promise was delayed, he needed to have more and more hope. But he doesn't give up hope, and he comforts himself by rereading the nobleman's letter that contained the promise. In this way he constantly comforts himself in his hope until he is confirmed in his confidence when the income arrives.

Just as this man accepted the delay by often rereading his letter, he kept himself buoyed up until the promise was fulfilled. So it is with us as we wait during the delay of Christ's second coming. It is by reading the Holy Scriptures that we confirm ourselves in the hope until at last we reach eternal life, which is promised us by Jesus Christ our Lord.

CHAPTER 6

THE CHRISTIAN'S VOCATION

Paul says to the Corinthians, 'Be ye imitators of me, as I am of Christ.' He meant by this, 'Imitate me, as you see I imitate Christ.' But had the Corinthians been spiritual, he would have said, 'Imitate me, and draw your picture from that which I have drawn of Christ.' Or he could have said to them as he said to the Ephesians, who were spiritual, 'Be ye imitators of God as dear children. Endeavor to recover the *image* and *likeness* of God, drawing it not from any man, but from God Himself.'

"It appears that Jesus Christ our Lord had the same object. On one occasion He said, 'Learn of me, for I am meek and lowly of heart' (Matt. 11:29). Elsewhere He says, 'Be ye perfect, as your Father in Heaven is perfect' (Matt. 5:48). You see, then, as I counsel you to draw the picture of the very image of Christ and of the very image of God, I am telling you no new and unrehearsed reality. It is something long known and realized by Christ Himself and by His apostle Paul. So apply it to yourselves also.

"Imitate David as far as he imitated God, was conformed in the image and likeness of God, and drew his picture from God Himself. Likewise, imitate Paul as he imitated Christ and was conformed to Christ Himself. But do not rest here. Pass onward and consider that you yourself have to draw your picture of life from the very image of Christ and of God Himself. The continual reading of the stories of Christ in the Gospels will help you do so. For then you will bring into personal effect the deeds and words of Christ. By them God shows great power in moving people's hearts, in mortifying them, and in renewing them, more than in any other words."

—From a *Letter of Juan de Valdés to Signora Donna Guilia Gonzaga*

THE CHRISTIAN'S VOCATION (XXVII)

The man who is called of God realizes and responds to this vocation. He will devote himself energetically to his faith, and he will do this first in regard to the world. He will refuse to have more of the world's dignities and esteem than should please God for him to have. He is moved as far as he is concerned not to desire any greater comforts for his material well-being or to be better off in outward circumstances than should please God for him to have.

I also understand that no man can maintain this resolution with reference to the world unless he also mortifies his inward affections, ambition, and all desires for personal significance. Nor will he be able to hold this resolution unless he is also able to mortify his sensual appetites. Once he perceives his vocation, he will be moved to make two resolutions.

The first is the perception of the reality of the faith to which he is called. The second is the presence of the Holy Spirit in his life which by faith is communicated to him. Together these will mortify the affections within him that might hinder or disturb his resolve to turn his back on the world and deny his lusts. Thus faith and the Holy Spirit will mortify a man's affections and lusts in order to maintain and uphold him in those resolves of his new vocation.

A devout person's feelings in being tempted by ambition and self-esteem are not necessarily a sign of being irresolute about his own self-discipline. It is a sign of not mortifying his lusts. From this I conclude that the devout person who responds to his vocation of being in Christ will form his resolve against the world as well as against himself. To sustain this resolve he will need to apply self-discipline seriously. Likewise, I understand that in the vocation of God to which a person feels called, he will also recognize the particular providence of God in all things that happen to him. For he will see that such events are all His doing; in them His will is done. So I recognize that the faith by which a man is called and the Holy Spirit by whom faith is communicated together help him to be content with whatever happens, whether it be good or evil. He will see it all to be good. So he is upheld and maintained in the assurance that he would not have been brought there without a purpose (Rom. 8:28–30).

Therefore when a devout soul anguishes at the bad things that have happened to him, it is not evidence that he is lacking assurance in the providence of God. It simply means that he has not yet brought all his mind to contentment with God's dealings with him. In addition to the application of self-discipline, the devout Christian must also bring his mind into conformity with the will of God. In doing this he will also maintain his assurance of God's providence. Then he will maintain himself in godliness, righteousness, and holiness, which are received by believing in Jesus Christ our Lord.

HOW TO BE SURE OF ONE'S VOCATION (II)

I believe it is of greatest importance for a person to be sure he has been called by God to the grace of the Gospel of Christ. He needs to realize that it is only by faith in Jesus Christ that he can have eternal life. This certainly gives him the right attitude toward the world and toward himself. And it is by spiritual self-discipline that his intent is maintained.

But what about someone who has not had a vocation as clear and evident as that of the apostle Paul when the Holy Spirit came upon him? And what about the disciples with whom Christ walked here on earth? And what about those people who were more affected inwardly by the Holy Spirit than outward efforts show?

What, then, is the way for some of us who may have inwardly known clearly this calling, but still find ourselves incapable of showing the calling in outward ways? How is such a person sure of his call?

I want to affirm that a person can have the certainty of his call not only outwardly but inwardly; this comes by his experience of justification by faith. Yes, he may doubt whether he has been moved by the call of God or by the stimulus of self-love when he is inclined and moved to cultivate Christian piety. He may say, "Which is it?" But if he experiences peace of conscience, then he will perceive the reality of justification by faith. By faith he makes the reality of God's righteousness his own. Such a person may then rest well-assured that his impulse was the call of God, and not simply his own human thoughts. It is certain that only those who are called by God will experience in themselves the benefit of the righteousness of God, which was executed upon Jesus Christ our Lord.

THE SIGN OF OUR VOCATION IS TO BELIEVE WITH DIFFICULTY (xxix)

People who believe very readily the tenets of Christian faith do so as a matter of opinion, of report from others, or of being readily persuaded by others. But the difficulty that other people have in believing comes in the area of inspiration and revelation. Thinking about this, I wonder whether those who believe only by hearsay things that are true are also very ready to believe many things that are not true. Indeed, they are even readier to believe what is untrue than what is true. Those who believe by revelation will believe only what is true and forget all that is false. The struggle to believe is itself a sign of vocation rather than a natural facility. He who believes by revelation can only believe as much as he has experienced. And because he finds contradictions in what he has not experienced, he will have to believe what is inspired and revealed to him. This is not always so, but when it is, then the revelation and the inspiration as well as the inward experience will be both vivid and complete.

Jesus calls those who have been given this faith "blessed." These indeed are the children of God. This is the faith that always has love and hope in its train. This is the faith without which it is impossible to please God (Heb. 11:6). This is the faith which cleanses, purifies, and quickens the heart. May our Almighty God enrich us with it, through Jesus Christ our Lord!

WHY DOES GOD UNFOLD OUR
VOCATION SO SLOWLY? (xxx)

Sometimes in my reckoning with God, I speak to Him like this. "Why is it, Lord, that when You call someone into Your Kingdom, he does not immediately experience his justification? Why do You not at once give him Your Holy Spirit to rule and to govern him? Why do You not at once assure him of Your presence?"

It seems to me that God's answer might be: "For the same reason that a farmer sowing the corn does not see it spring up at once; it takes time for it to be harvested."

This, I will argue, is because of the curse of sin. God replies, "The slowness of our spiritual growth is likewise the result of the curse of sin."

My response is, "Since You worked so dramatically with the apostle Paul and others, why do You not deal the same way with other people?"

His reply is, "For the same reason that I have at times given men bread miraculously without it having been produced in the normal way. In both ways I also show My omnipotence."

"But is it not true, Lord, that those to whom You gave bread in a miraculous way are more grateful for that bread? They see it is derived from Your evident bounty more than those who receive it daily in an ordinary fashion. Likewise, would not all the elect be more grateful to You for inward gifts if You were to deal with them as You did with the apostle Paul? Or if you were to guide them as dramatically as You did rather than in the ordinary fashion?"

"It is My will," God replies, "that both should be grateful to Me whether they receive in a normal or an unusual manner. Indeed, it is My will in this matter that they rather acquire things by hard effort and discipline, so that they will also mortify the judgment of their human wisdom. For they would do without self-discipline if they were to receive these things from Me in a miraculous way.

"It is My will that the laborer should cultivate the earth and sow the seed in order that he might attribute to Me the fruit of his labors. Likewise, it is My will that spiritual persons should strive and labor and surrender themselves to faith and to love that they may obtain justification and the presence of the Holy Spirit. It is also My will that they attribute it all to Me.

"A cultivator can anticipate a large harvest if he realizes that he has water at his disposal and all the sunshine that he needs. Likewise, a spiritual person will progress greatly in godliness when he has divine inspiration at his command whenever he needs it. Be sure of this, then, that the spiritual person understands best when he freely resigns himself to Me without any struggle and without a thought of self-will. Then he will be controlled wholly by Me."

With such reflections, I set my mind at rest whenever I find it is getting impatient and little disposed to meet with God. Then I commit myself to God in everything and in every way. For I am assured that He governs man, and He will govern me in this Christian matter just as much as my need requires, by His only begotten Son, Jesus Christ our Lord.

THE PASSION OF AMBITION (LII)

I realize that Jesus Christ our Lord tells all of us who are Christians to learn "lowliness of heart from Him" (Matt. 11:29). I also understand from the apostle Paul that we should "subject our minds to what we recognize to be in our Lord Jesus Christ, who being the Son of God humbled Himself so much as to take the form of a servant, and made Himself man" (Phil. 2:5–8). Just as humility of mind is the most profitable thing for a Christian, so likewise the passion of ambition of one's self is the opposite. For it is this spirit of self-ambition which is most pernicious, and which separates the Christian most from Christ, and which identifies man as belonging to Satan.

I see this passion of ambition in every desire, every thought, and every effort that is exerted by man in order to increase his own self-fulfillment, his own reputation and honor, and his own hold upon all the possessions that he has acquired. So this passion of ambition has two aspects to it: One is acquisitiveness and the other is possessiveness.

Ordinary wisdom judges those who limit their acquisition as free from the passion of ambition. Indeed, they are to a large extent free from it. But they will still be possessive, a more difficult trait to get rid of since human wisdom is not recognized as evil. But the Holy Spirit does recognize it as an evil and judges those to be ambitious who have it. He desires that those whom He rules be completely free of it. They should renounce it and free themselves from it so that they will never desire promotion in the eyes of the world, nor be preoccupied with the way they may get it. Although God does not demand by their deeds and at their own initiative that they should do things which will degrade and impair their position and reputation, yet He will train their minds to be content with whatever they have according to the will of God. He also wills that they seek in everything and everywhere to increase in the favor of God's eyes and to hold on to what they have gained.

For this reason, the devout Christian learns humility through Christ. He will seek to bring himself into conformity with Christ in His humility. He will be convinced of the need to quench the fires of ambition. He will then take from his mind every thought that aims at promotion in the affairs of the world. He will also discipline instincts of self-possessiveness for the things which he has acquired. He will anticipate the things of God, in his trusting, hoping, and loving. He will also endeavor to maintain himself in all the divine confidence, hope, and love that he will receive from God.

Inwardly, the devout one will resolve that what remains for him to do is to simply please God and to possess His Spirit. He will therefore not seek the world nor those who adopt the opinions and counsels of human wisdom. In doing so, he will become like Jesus Christ our Lord.

WHY IS LOVE SUPREME? (LXX)

The apostle Paul places faith, hope, and love among the highest and most excellent of God's gifts. I have often wondered in what this supremacy consists. I do not seem to be able to realize why love has this preeminence.

I understand what faith consists of. It is what a man believes and holds for certain in all that is contained in the Holy Scriptures. He places his trust in the divine promises within Scripture as if they were distinctively and primarily given to himself.

If we think of the distinction between the two parts of faith as belief and confidence, I conclude that the human mind is capable to some extent of belief. By this I mean that a man who is self-sufficient can force himself to believe or to persuade himself that he does believe.

But I find man is incapable of having confidence. For he is not self-sufficient to bring himself to this confidence or persuade himself that he does have this confidence. He who believes, and yet does not have confidence, shows that his belief is the result only of mental effort and human ability. It does not come from divine inspiration. But he who believes in confidence shows that his belief is due to inspiration and revelation. From this I gather that faith is a good test whereby a man may know that his belief is due to inspiration and revelation and so be truly assured.

I mean by hope that one has patience and endurance. A man who believes and confides will also await the fulfillment of God's promises. This he can do without putting himself at the disposal of Satan, or yearning for the vanity of this world, or deliberately doing either in his own fleshly lusts.

A man with hope is like an officer who has been promised by the emperor that, on his arrival in Italy, he will give him a commission. Although the emperor delays to do so and the officer is solicited by many other princes who would like to have his services, he declines to accept any terms. Awaiting the emperor's arrival, he is afraid that should the ruler come and find him in the service of another, he might be unwilling to employ him.

This hope presupposes faith. To wait involves a necessary faith on the part of him who so hopes. For it is in this way he will give credit for what has been said to him and place trust in what has been promised to him. Otherwise he could not keep up his expectation. Such hope really consists in such parables of the Gospel as the ten virgins who await the Bridegroom, that is, who await their Lord's return (Matt. 25:1–13).

I understand that love consists in affection. A man who believes in faith and is tested in hope will bear love toward God and Christ. Similarly, he bears things of God in Christ while being peculiarly attracted and enamored by faith, hope, and love. The man who has these three gifts of God is united to God in believing, hoping, and loving. It is with profound reason that these three gifts are ranked above all others as the most excellent gifts.

Now that we understand what these three gifts of God mean and also what constitutes their preeminence, we also desire to understand why the same apostle places love above faith and hope as the greatest (1 Cor. 13:13). I understand and I hold for certain that the preeminence consists of this. Whoever believes and confides will never be firm in faith unless he finds pleasure and relaxation in believing and confiding. Nor will he who hopes be able to be firm in hope unless he also finds joy and blessing in such hope.

Love, then, is that which gives taste and relish to sustain faith and hope. It plainly follows that love is more eminent than faith and hope, while at the same time it sustains these others. Unaided they would not be able to maintain and support themselves. Love maintains and sustains the others, which will also reciprocally maintain and support love. But faith will fail when there is nothing to believe or confide in. Likewise, hope will fail when Christ has come again and the resurrection of the just has been accomplished. There will remain nothing more to hope.

But love will never fail because it will always have objects to love, and it will always have what it can enjoy. For in eternal life we shall love God in Christ. We shall find pleasure and relish in the contemplation of God in Christ. We, who in this life have lived in faith, hope, and love, will be united in Jesus Christ our Lord.

HUMAN AND SPIRITUAL WISDOM IN SUFFERING

Human wisdom believes it is humility not to trust God, and that it is arrogant to confide in Him. With such an attitude, the Christian must always be on his guard so that he does not sell white for black, nor sell black for white. So when a devout Christian is overtaken with some great trial or grief, he may be tempted by the Devil through human wisdom to believe it is wrong to feel that God cares for him. That is, it is wrong to believe God will deliver him from his grief and trial. With this temptation comes the attitude that it is the Christian's duty to simply be content with whatever God may appoint him to go through.

At first sight, this attitude seems devout and pious. But when it is examined by a Christian spirit, there is despair and distrust recognized in it. For it rests on the assumption that it is wrong to trust God.

The second assumption concerning mental submission may be good, but it is spoiled by the first attitude. Now in order to have the right attitude of acceptance, the Christian spirit must establish the first assumption about trust on a good basis. That is to say, every devout soul in grief and trouble must be persuaded that God has promised to honor those who trust Him. He will not allow them to be misused by the world, but He will assist them and defend them in His care for them.

Do you honor God? Then you can be assured and certain that God will honor you, and that He will deliver you from the grief and trouble in which you are involved. By this principle all God's promises in the Holy Scriptures can fill the Christian's mind. When the saint is under trial, and yet holds this truth, he will remain steadfast and firm. This hope will encourage him to attune his mind to God's purpose in the trial. In such a case, submission to the divine will is pious and holy because it is based on a confidence that is in itself pious and holy.

But human wisdom is opposed to this. It will argue that it is evident God has permitted His people to be persecuted, afflicted, and mistreated. How, then, can you be confident as a Christian that He will deliver you from this affliction and travail?

To this a Christian spirit replies, "Yes, it is true that God permits all this to happen to His people. But He does so when it is calculated to promote the cause of the Gospel, the manifestation of His glory, or the glorification of His name. For it is not intended to gratify the evil and basic desires of men in the world. Yes, God does allow His saints to be mistreated. When they are so tested it is because they are saints. It is from such testings that the consequences will follow which we have described. But He does not allow them to be mistreated for evil motives, because He has promised in His Word to do just the opposite."

David exults in that he, throughout the course of his life, had never seen a righteous man abandoned by God (Ps. 37:25). Consequently, all the righteous may exult for the same reason. Although God will permit them to suffer, they suffer as saints and righteously so. He does not allow them to suffer under circumstances which are irrelevant to this present life.

We may conclude that when a Christian is mistreated for his righteousness and piety, he can and should submit himself and all his fears into the hands of God. He should let his mind acquiesce in all that God may ordain for him. Let him rejoice that God's name will thus be magnified in and by such suffering. But when a Christian is badly treated as a man of the world, he can believe and be assured that God will deliver him from that grief and trouble to his own great satisfaction and content. And he ought to bring his mind to be satisfied with the way in which God shall deal with him. This, then, is the truly Christian disposition of mind. It is only found in those who are united in Jesus Christ our Lord.

HOW TO DEAL WITH SPIRITUAL ARIDITY (XXIII)

However, I sometimes find my mind is sterile and dried out. It is as if it were alienated from God. I believe that this comes when God hides His presence from me. I thought that I could remedy this simply by being occupied with the meditations of God alone. But I had scarcely attempted to do this when I realized the following: While I can think upon Him as I can about anything else, it is still not in my power to cause my mind to *feel* the presence of God, and thus to free it from the sense of barrenness, aridity, and alienation from God.

I have also realized what an utter difference there is between the state of the soul when it tries to experience the presence of God and the state when God Himself makes me conscious of His presence. Seeking to know what this difference consists of, I have observed that in the first instance, it is merely the operation of the human mind. In the other instance, when God makes me conscious of His presence, it is the presence of the Holy Spirit. So I have come to the conclusion that the same difference exists between these two states of mind as exists between the flesh and the Spirit.

Thinking further, I have come to see that the men who, for their own self-seeking and purpose, seek and strive to separate themselves from the world and to set their affections upon God are neither inspired nor moved to do so by the Holy Spirit. Although they may resemble those who are doing it generally, it is still an artificial unreality. They will therefore never succeed in reaching their goal.

Again, I understand that God would separate us from the world and enamor us with Himself. He is like someone of high rank who has designed to attach Himself to those who are of a much lower station in society than Himself. Both parties can have the same feelings and emotions that stimulate affections between them. But all the initiative comes from the One who has stooped to pay such attentions.

This is very different from those who love each other in a compatible way. There is always the uncertainty that the compatible relationship may cease. But the One who stoops and continues to stoop deliberately enables the other to realize that however he may feel or respond, the relationship is always in the hands of the Other who remains ever loyal and constant. Therefore, the Christian in his relationship will always feel wholly freed from any fear.

The Christian whom God would separate from the world is enabled by God to fall in love with Him. Seeing this, he will apply himself diligently and exercise himself in every way to be more deeply in love with God. He will then experience in himself that he finds it necessary to detach himself from the purposes and interests of the world in order to be more deeply in love with God.

I also understand that they may regard themselves as most fortunate who know that they are not self-motivated to detach themselves from the world to be attached to God. For unless they have been moved by the Spirit of God, they cannot be so detached from the world. Such, I realize, are only wasting their efforts if they are not being moved to love by God's Spirit, or if God chooses to hide His presence from them. Then their own efforts and diligence to compensate for this are useless. God, in holding Himself aloof from them, may do so to show that seeking His presence may only be out of self-interest after all!

Above all, I understand it is the duty of those whom God has pleased to disenchant with the world and to love Him to apply their minds to this disenchantment. Let them do so neither desiring the world's favors, its caresses, nor its attractions. Rather let them avoid and abominate them all.

It is indeed by God's favors to them that they are stripped and deprived of worldly favors. He does so in order that they may more effectively penetrate more deeply and be more transformed into God's likeness. Then they will be able readily and quickly to experience the love of God. This truth is like the experience of a highly gifted person who totally desists from any intercourse and conversation with someone who is vulgar and base.

As I have reflected on these considerations, I have referred them to Holy Scripture, and I find them to be quite in harmony with what I read there. In the Song of Songs, Solomon celebrates the love of God and the soul. But he speaks also of the separation that takes place when the soul leaves God and devotes itself to the world; this is called adultery.

It appears to me that the conduct of our Lord Jesus Christ, both in declining to allow someone to follow Him and in calling another who argued for a delay because of a difficulty (Matt. 8:21), did nothing else than to reject the love of the one and desire to gain the love of the other. This, I believe, He gave the apostles to help them understand when He said to them, "You have not chosen Me, but I have chosen you" (John 15:16). It is as if He had said, you did not set your affections upon Me, but I have set Mine upon you.

I understand that the apostle John expresses the same idea of God's divine initiative when he says that to be a son of God, one must become so neither by the will of the flesh, nor by the will of man, but by the will of God and through the Holy Spirit (John 1:13).

Thus man in this present world must strive to disenchant himself with the world and remain in love with Him. Then he will receive from Him to the end the Holy Spirit, which is attainable in faith, through Jesus Christ our Lord.

CHAPTER 7

THE BENEFITS OF A JUSTIFIED LIFE IN CHRIST

For they being ignorant of God's righteousness, and going about to establish their own righteousness, have not submitted themselves to the righteousness of God" (Rom. 10:3).

"This sentence is most divine. It is most worthy to be considered in opposition to human wisdom, which always seeks its own self-justification. For here the apostle Paul states that, for this reason, the zeal of the Jews was not according to knowledge. Being ignorant of God's righteousness, they sought to justify themselves by their own works and virtuous life. Thus they did not submit themselves to the righteousness of God. Generally these words also apply to all who seek self-justification by their own works....

"Every Christian should be watchful to recognize the same tendency in himself and to seek ways and means to deal with it. Indeed, every Christian should view all his actions with deep distrust, especially those which have the outward appearance of goodness and piety.

"By 'the righteousness of God' I understand then the way in which God is most just and perfect in Himself. Those who are ignorant of the righteousness of God are unaware that the righteousness of man must have the same exalted character if man is to be accepted by God as just. But those who know the righteousness of God are only too well aware that all the aggregate of universal innocence that a man might pretend to live with would not suffice (even if it ever existed) to account such a man just before God.

"So those who are ignorant of God's righteousness go around to establish their own righteousness ... and do not submit to the righteousness of God.... In this they only show how ignorant of God's righteousness they really are. For if they knew it they would despair of their ability ever to justify themselves by their works, and instead they would submit themselves to the righteousness of God.

"On the other hand, those who have renounced their own righteousness testify about themselves that they realize how just God is. Knowing it, they have despaired of themselves. So they have placed their reliance before God. From this it may be concluded that only the just know God as just. And only those are just who have renounced their own righteousness to submit themselves to the righteousness of God, because they alone are justified by the righteousness of Christ. The apostle Paul is warranted in calling it 'the righteousness of God,' because it is by it, and with it, that God justifies."

—From the *Commentary on the Epistle to the Romans*

THE BENEFITS OF CHRIST'S OBEDIENCE (CVIII)

From what I read in Holy Scripture and from what I know of myself, I understand it to be fundamental to believe in the benefit of Christ's obedience.... For it is in Christ's obedience we have all obeyed, and it is in His resurrection that we have all been raised. As a corollary of this, we need to realize also that it is in Adam's disobedience that we have all disobeyed, and in Adam's death that we have all died.

I say it is necessary for each one to believe in the evil that has been wrought by Adam in order to be brought to believe in the benefit wrought by Christ. It is impossible to believe the one without the other. For no one will ever come to believe in the benefit of Christ, which is the proper medicine, without recognizing the specific injury done by Adam.

From this I learned two things. The first is that man, by believing in the injury done by Adam, frees himself from that injury; but by believing in the benefit conferred by Christ, he enjoys that benefit. So it is the duty of everyone to believe both in that injury and in that benefit. However, this is not merely hoping to feel it in order to believe in it. For this would invert the order established by God, who wills that we believe before we feel.

The other thing that I learned is that those who do not surrender themselves to live as dead and as made alive by Christ do not believe that they have died in Adam or that they have risen again in Christ. However much they may declare and affirm their belief in both of these things, there is no doubt that they labor to live as those who, having been dead, have been made alive.

The granting of a pardon that a king may extend to those who are in exile because of some crime is sufficient cause for those pardoned to leave the foreign kingdom and its service and return to their own kingdom under the service of their own king. Likewise the offer of the Gospel is sufficient to cause all who accept it to leave the kingdom of the world and its service and to enter into the Kingdom of God and His service. Seeking to live after the flesh, we now should live after the Spirit. This is what God wills, that we should leave the kingdom of the world and its service, and come to the Kingdom of God. We come to serve God in holiness and righteousness and in the Gospel of His only begotten Son, Jesus Christ our Lord.

THE BENEFITS OF CHRIST'S ASSURANCE (XVI)

Christian piety emphasizes with certainty and assurance that God is committed to uphold a believer by His grace in this life and in the life to come and give him immortality and glory. Human wisdom, in an assumed form of piety, will try to persuade the Christian that he ought to feel assured God will do all this for him on the condition that he has enough faith, hope, and love.

Human wisdom does not seem to realize that faith, hope, and love are the gifts of God that are imparted to the Christian, and that the extent of a man's possession of these three gifts will be relative to his assurance and certainty. The Christian needs, then, to stop his ears to human wisdom and to open them to the promises of the Holy Spirit. The devout Christian knows that God only calls those to Himself whom He had first known and predestinated. Again, the devout one knows that those whom God calls, them He also justifies and glorifies.

Let him hold this and remain assured of it, never doubting in the least. For the promises of God are fulfilled to all such believers. Many passages of Scripture may be cited to prove this, but it is better to conclude it as follows. The truth of this is not believed unless it is first experienced. This experience belongs only to those who are incorporated in Jesus Christ our Lord.

WHY OTHERS DO NOT RECOGNIZE THE BENEFITS OF CHRIST (CVII)

The more deeply I meditate upon the benefits of Christ and recognize that He is in all things, the more I marvel that all do not go after, embrace, and enthrone Him in their hearts. For forgiveness and reconciliation with God, and consequently eternal life, are offered freely to them in Christ. As I wonder why they do not accept the matchless grace He offers, I realize that its nonacceptance comes from man's ignorance both of himself and of God.

Since man is unconscious of his rebellion, which through original sin is natural to him, man does not distrust himself as to his own personal ability to satisfy God and to be just before Him. Likewise, since man does not recognize the goodness, mercy, and faithfulness of God, he distrusts Him. So he cannot be assured in his mind that the righteousness of Christ really can belong to him, or that God can accept him as righteous on account of what Christ has suffered.

And if man does not know himself as a sinner, then he does not know how to distrust himself concerning his own self-justification. And if he but knew God, and recognized in Him goodness, mercy, and faithfulness, he would readily trust Him and accept the pardon and much more which the Gospel offers to him. So that is why I see it is impossible for man, when he neither knows himself nor God, to accept the truth. Nor can he accept the grace of the Gospel, or depend upon it.

What then about the Jewish saints when they attempted to justify themselves through the sacrifices that were prescribed by the Law? I answer that the Jewish saints did not base their righteousness upon their sacrifices, but upon the Word of God that promised to pardon them upon the basis of sacrifices.

God no longer asks men to offer sacrifices in order to have reconciliation with Him and the remission of sin. For He has laid upon Christ the sins of all. So I must either know myself to be righteous in Christ, even though I recognize myself to be a sinner in myself, or else I will deny what the Gospel affirms, that God has borne upon Christ the iniquities of us all. Otherwise I am constrained to say that God is unjust, punishing sins twice over: once in Christ and again in me. Since this would be an act of impiety to say this (and to deny the other would be an act of infidelity), it remains that I am constrained to recognize myself as pardoned by and reconciled to God, and thus justified in Christ.

I also learned this. Since the impossibility that man finds in accepting this holy Gospel of Christ proceeds from his ignorance of himself and of God, it is every man's duty to earnestly know himself and his natural inclinations as derived from Adam, as well as to know God. This he can do by continually praying to God affectionately and fervently that He will open the eyes of his mind so that he will have both these kinds of knowledge. In this way, if he has not commenced to accept the holy Gospel of Christ, then he will begin to accept it. And as he does so, the difficulty will be removed.

For it is by these things that the Christian faith is confirmed in us which serves as the foundation to that confession of the apostle Peter. He said to Christ: "Thou art the Christ, the Son of the living God" (Matt. 16:16). To Him be glory ever more. Amen.

THE DOCTRINE OF ATONEMENT (LXXII)

I have often heard people speak of the agony, fear, horror, and sorrow that Jesus Christ our Lord felt in His passion and death. They have pretended to explain why Christ felt His suffering and death so intensely. Yet many others have suffered and died, some without evincing much feeling. Others have not shown any at all. Others again apparently rejoice and delight in their suffering and even in their death. Having never been satisfied in my own mind with the explanations that I have heard, I meditated on what I heard a preacher say with regard to the passages of Isaiah 53 and 1 Peter 2.

I came to this conclusion. God laid all our sins on Christ. In order to chastise them all in Himself, He took them all upon Himself, and having known them in general and in particular, He felt for each of them that confusion, shame, and grief that He would have felt had He Himself committed them all. Seeing Himself in the presence of God so contaminated and polluted with so many and such abominable sins, He thus felt all the agony, all the fear, all that inward sorrow, all that shame and confusion that would have fallen to the lot of each one of us to feel for each of our own sins had we been so chastised for them.

Hence it was that He sweated drops of blood in the garden with the agony that He felt. This was not because He saw Himself about to die, but because He saw Himself in the presence of God laden with so many sins. It was on this account that He prayed with His face to the earth. He prayed as a man would pray who should be ashamed to look up to heaven, a man who knew that he was burdened with so many offenses perpetrated against God.

Truly this is the reason Christ expressed far greater feelings of sorrow in His passion and death than did any one of the martyrs who suffered for the sake of the Gospel or any one of the men of the world who died from secular motives. A man who should find himself in the presence of some mighty prince and interceding for the pardon of one who had acted a traitor toward him may have felt some small spark of the shame and confusion which Christ felt in seeing Himself polluted with our sins.

Now it is true that God has laid all our sins upon Christ, and that Christ has taken them all upon Himself, so one can understand what Isaiah says, when he says: "He has borne our griefs and carried our sorrows" (Isa. 53:4). And again further on he says, "He was scourged for our transgressions, and He was beaten for our iniquities" (v. 5). And further on, "He bore the sin of many" (v. 12).

In the same way, the apostle Peter expresses himself. "For even hereunto were ye called: because Christ also suffered for us, leaving us an example, that ye should follow his steps: Who did not sin, neither was guile found in his mouth: Who, when he was reviled, reviled not again; when he suffered, he threatened not; but committed himself to him that judgeth righteously." (1 Peter 2:21–23 KJV).

Here I understand two most important things. The first is that if the rigor of the righteousness which was executed upon Christ, outwardly as well as inwardly, had been executed upon us all (each one getting his own desert for his own offenses of sins), then we all should have gone to perdition. For none of us would be equal to bear upon himself the chastisement that he should have had to suffer had Christ not satisfied the justice of God for us. Therefore, Caiaphas rightly said (and if he had only rightly felt it): "It is expedient for us, that one man should die for the people and the whole nation should perish not" (John 11:50).

The other thing that I understand from this is that it was more necessary that He should be more than man. Indeed it was necessary that He should be the Son of God who had to reconcile men with God by having to be chastised for the sins of all. Knowing and feeling Himself charged with them all, just as if He had committed them all, He and only He had to be able to stand up against all the agony, fear, sadness, shame, and confusion without giving way and so failing in obedience to God.

Because He persevered and He stood steadfast and constant in His mission, He is compared to a lamb that is led to the slaughter

(Isa. 53:7). This is as much on account of the innocence of His life as of the obedience that He demonstrated by being sacrificed for us. As the Son of God, One in the same essence with God, such was His obedience. Such it is and such it will be. To Him be glory and honor forevermore. Amen.

ONLY THE CHILDREN OF GOD HAVE SATISFACTION IN EVERYTHING (XCI)

No one can reach a conclusion except in one of three ways. (This applies to devotion as it does to everything else.) One will conclude voluntarily, involuntarily, or by the grace of God. In those things to which we come voluntarily, there is design. In those things to which we come involuntarily, there is suffering. In those things to which we come by the grace of God, there is admiration.

The children of Adam never find any certain or solid satisfaction in the things of piety to which they arrive by design. Designs are based on self-interest and self-love. Having this basis, when their design fails them, they can never experience satisfaction, however much they may persuade themselves that they are satisfied and wish to appear so before others. But such is the fact that those persons know by personal experience who willingly desire piety and change their mode of life, their career and condition, and will occupy or exert themselves more in one thing than in another.

But the children of God find their satisfaction in the things at which they arrive voluntarily and with purpose when their design is to promote the denial of self and the life in Christ. They do this by the grace of God and in serving Christ in His members. This is true for those who know it by personal experience, esteeming themselves dead by the cross of Christ; these are intent upon mortification. Their desire to mortify themselves is only in order to live as being dead, since "they are dead and their life is hid with Christ in God" (Col. 3:3).

The children of Adam are seldom free from suffering and grief in the things that occur to them involuntarily. Such things are troubles, sicknesses, death, and dishonor because they ignore the will of God in these things. Or if they recognize it to be so, they hold it to be rigorous, and therefore consider themselves to be the enemies of God. Such is the fact that we almost all know more or less by experience.

But the children of God are free from suffering and grief in the things that occur to them involuntarily, when they recognize the will of God in them. Then they will seek to conform themselves to their condition. In this conformity, they find contentment and satisfaction of mind. They do so, even though the flesh feels pain and suffering, and they are in a predicament that they would not seek for themselves. It is therefore no surprise that the flesh under such circumstances revolts and suffers, for it revolts and suffers in the person of the only begotten Son of God, Jesus Christ our Lord.

The children of Adam are seldom brought by God's grace under the influence of divine things. When they are so, they neither feel it, nor recognize it; so they do not relish these things. Not relishing them, they cannot find any inward satisfaction in them. This is true for those who as the children of Adam are now the children of God. They can recall those occasions when they were brought by God's grace. But they did not recognize God's grace within them, and felt neither relish nor satisfaction in them.

But the children of God are frequently brought by God's grace under the influence of divine things, and when they feel and recognize them they relish them. Relishing them, they find satisfaction therein and are lost in admiration. This is true because the children of God themselves experience how frequently they have been brought to many things, without personal desire or design, and yet do so without contradiction and without suffering. By the marvelous grace of God, they find themselves abhorring those things which they previously loved, and loving those things that they previously hated, without being aware in what way or how they were led to do so.

This marvelous and gracious work, as I understand it, God brings about in His children in the following ways.

First, this work opens their eyes to recognize Christ's righteousness. Because He shows them that it belongs to them, it causes them to abhor their own self-righteousness. By this I mean all these things men do in striving to justify themselves in the sight of God. From such ways they have wholly ceased and now despise and condemn them.

Second, it opens their eyes to the recognition of His deity. He draws them to a knowledge of themselves and of the men of the world. In this way, He disenchants them of themselves and of the world, and enamors them concerning Himself in Christ.

Third, it opens their eyes to the knowledge that God by slaying Christ upon the cross slew their flesh at the same time. Thus He leads them to hate their own flesh, and so He brings it to pass that, with inward resolution, they love mortification and strive to achieve it.

Fourth, it opens their eyes to the blissful reality of eternal life. Through the consideration of Christ risen, He leads them to hate this present life and all that is in it and belongs to it. In this way, they learn to love eternal life and despise this present life; yea, they rejoice in parting with it.

Finally, God, when He wills to bring His children to hate an evil thing, gives them the knowledge of a good thing. He knows that they, seeing some good, will spurn the evil much more quickly than if He had only given them to see the evil. For example, I will bring myself much more quickly and with more alacrity to hate the worldly life by considering the blessedness of a Christian life than I would by merely considering the evil of a worldly life. This I understand is the result of the natural constitution of the human heart: It can never cease to love something. In order to bring it to hate what it loves, it is necessary that some other thing be proposed to it that it may love instead.

In this discourse there are, as I understand it, nine principal things.

- The first is that the children of Adam find no certain or solid satisfaction in anything. The children of God find it in everything they do, because they are the children of God.
- The second is that my purpose will then be a Christian one when what I do voluntarily will show an increase of the grace of God.
- The third is that my mind will have cause for contentment and satisfaction, in what comes to me involuntarily, even though the flesh may revolt and suffer.
- The fourth is that in those things into which I find myself transported without consciousness of purpose on my part, or by violence on that of others, those things I am to recognize as from the gracious hand of God.
- The fifth is that God, by giving me the knowledge of spiritual things in their eternal and true nature, leads me to hate things which in their nature are material, temporal, and false.
- The sixth is that by recognizing myself dead on the cross of Christ, I render mortification easy.
- The seventh is that by desiring to know God, I also learn to know the world and myself, and to abhor both the world and my natural self.
- The eighth is that in attaining the knowledge of Christ's righteousness, I will renounce and reject every thought of self-justification.
- The ninth is that those who have not begun to hate every kind of self-justification, themselves, their work, this present life, and things temporal and false have not yet begun to be the children of God. They remain as the children of Adam. While those who are even only beginning to be the children of God will begin to feel the germs of all these enmities to which they are incited. For the children of God are they who, believing in the Gospel, are incorporated into the only begotten Son of God, Jesus Christ our Lord.

THREE BASES OF CONSCIENCE (xciv)

I understand that every man upon earth molds his conscience upon one of three bases.

First, there are some who mold their conscience by attending to natural religion. This consists of a man wholly devoting himself and every member of his body to those things for which he knows God created him and them. He avails himself of all created things specifically for the purposes God had in creating them. Such mold their consciences upon the law of nature, forming a good or bad judgment of themselves to the degree they see their life harmonize with, or vary from, the dictates of natural religion.

I understand that the more these people have their minds illumined to know the extent to which they are brought under obligation to natural religion, the more they endeavor to discharge that obligation. Then they form so much the worse opinion of themselves. They know that they fail in many ways to perform the duties of natural religion. Because of the depravity of natural religion, however, man can never discharge himself righteously.

Second, there are others who attend to the Jewish religion. This consists of a man living in every way conformable to those laws by which he is obliged, or by which he persuades himself that he is obliged. He tries to observe them according to the intention of their Maker. These mold their consciences upon what they know of these laws and entertain a good or bad opinion of themselves to the degree they see that their life concurs with, or varies from, the demands of those laws.

I understand that the more such persons realize the extent to which they are bound by these laws, and the more that they study to fulfill that obligation, so much the worse opinion will they have about themselves. But they know that they will fail often in the many duties of the Jewish religion that they long to be able to do. Yet it is impossible for them to do so. This is because of the blindness of their intellect. For they cannot fathom the peculiar design of Him who made the laws. Not knowing the laws in their fullness, they can never be assured that they have satisfied them. Another reason for their failure is the rebellion of the flesh. As the apostle Paul says in Romans 8:7, "It is not subject to the law of God, nor indeed can be."

Third, there are those who hear the voice of the Gospel that promises remission of sins and reconciliation with God to those who believe in Christ. Such have ceased to profess natural religion and also repudiate the claims of the Jewish religion. Instead, they embrace the Christian faith, which simply consists in this: A man is incorporated by faith into Christ. As such, he can regard himself as pious, just, and holy, although he does not wholly satisfy either natural religion or the Jewish religion. At the same time, he does not wholly satisfy the duties and claims of the Christian faith.

I understand that the more such persons have their minds illumined by the knowledge of the Gospel of Christ, the more they will study to give credit to the Gospel, and so much the better opinion they will have of themselves. But they form judgment not upon what they know of themselves, but by what they believe of the Gospel. God does not consider them in the light of what they are in themselves, but by what they are in Christ. He does not judge them to be good or bad by the degree to which they approach to, or diverge from, the duties of the natural religion or of the Jewish religion, nor indeed by the measure to which they maintain Christian standards. Nor does God judge them by what they fail to do, nor by the faithfulness or the unfaithfulness of their own perseverance. He judges them by the provisions of the Gospel of Christ.

People who practice natural religion, since they are destitute of the Christian faith, are apt to be vicious, because the flesh operates licentiously in them.

People who observe the Jewish religion, since they are also destitute of the Christian faith, are apt to be superstitious and over-scrupulous. All their scruples and doubts they call cases of conscience. Unable to completely understand the purpose of the Law-giver, they are unable to have assurance that they have satisfied the Law. So they persist in striving to satisfy the Law by superstitious observance. Beset with the deepest scruples, they seek to comply with all the prerequisites of the Jewish religion. As they try to comply, they become the more frustrated. So long as a man remains subject to the Law and forms his conscience from the opinion he has of himself, he will never come to experience peace of conscience.

But those who come to the Christian faith mold their consciences upon the opinion that God has of them. They see themselves as united in Christ; this is not according to what they know of themselves. The more the Christian faith dominates their life, the more they will clearly see the falsities of natural religion and of the Jewish religion. They will not mold their consciences to their own standards of satisfaction. Instead, they will live the dictates of the Christian faith and of the spirit of the Gospel.

Such people alone are not carnal because the flesh does not work in them. Indeed, since they are dead on the cross with Christ, their conscience will be gradually mortified. They alone are freed from superstitious and overscrupulous fears because they know that Christ has released them wholly from the Law. They know that it has been satisfied on their behalf. Being free, they no longer have anyone to accuse them. Because they also know that God does not impute to them their failure to live the Christian faith and act according to the Christian Gospel, they affectionately desire to be like God and like the Son of God Himself, Jesus Christ our Lord.

IS JUSTIFICATION THE FRUIT OF PIETY OR IS PIETY THE FRUIT OF JUSTIFICATION? (XCVII)

Which of these two fruits of God—piety or justification—may be said to be the fruit of the other? Is piety the fruit of justification, of man being just before he is pious, or is justification the fruit of piety, of man being pious before he is just?

To proceed in sequence in this inquiry, let me say first of all that by piety I mean true divine worship that consists of worshiping God "in Spirit and in truth" (John 4:24). By this I mean mentally approving all that God does and holding it to be just, holy, and good. It is in this sense that I understand the apostle Paul uses the word "piety" or godliness (1 Tim. 3:16).

By justification I mean the purity of conscience which dares to appear before the judge, such as was the experience of the apostle Paul when he said, "There is laid up for me a crown of righteousness" (2 Tim. 4:8).

If one were to answer this question in the light of what is natural, prudent, and humanly wise, the answer would always be that justification is the fruit of piety; this assumes that a man cannot be justified and pure in his conscience unless he first worships God "in Spirit and in truth." That is to say that he renders God that which he as His creature owes Him. But as he renders to God what he owes to Him, then he is just and his conscience is cleansed. The conclusion may thus appear to be that justification is the fruit of piety since it results from a man's being pious before he is just.

But if I judge according to the counsel of the Holy Spirit and of the Spirit of Christ, I will find God affirming that piety is the fruit of justification. It is the realization that a man cannot have piety and worship God "in Spirit and in truth" unless he is previously made just. This is to say that, unless he accepts the Gospel of Christ and appropriates the righteousness of Christ, and understands that as soon as he becomes just by believing he begins to be godly—only then can he worship God "in Spirit and in truth." God would conclude that piety is the fruit of justification, because a man is just prior to his being godly.

If the light of nature, prudence, and human reason were true, it would follow from that rationale that there has never been, or is, or ever will be, a godly man. That is to say, there will never be one who is perfectly and truly rendering to God what he owes Him.

But after making certain what the Holy Spirit and the Spirit of Christ declare, it rightly follows that there have been, there are, and there will be, a great number of just people. For such have accepted and appropriated their righteousness in Christ.

Those who assume justification to be the fruit of godliness show that they judge by the light of nature, prudence, and human reason as Plato and Aristotle would have judged; that is, those who never heard of Christ. In truth I know not what they feel respecting Christ, or the affairs of Christ, or of the Gospel.

But those who judge piety to be the fruit of justification witness by doing so that they judge by the Holy Spirit and by the Spirit of Christ. They follow the apostles Peter and Paul who knew Christ profoundly and who possessed the Spirit of Christ.

Such men form the opinion of Christ that God has punished all our sins in Him. All in which we fail and all we justly owe God as His creatures are taken care of by the remission of sins and justification by Christ on the one hand, and the rule and government of the Holy Spirit on the other. These two realities they enjoy; by believing in Christ they accept the Gospel.

From all of this it may be gathered that they who understand justification to be the fruit of piety follow the reasoning of Plato and Aristotle, while those who understand piety to be the fruit of justification (which itself is the fruit of faith) follow in the teachings of the apostles Paul and Peter.

It is also to be understood from this that this word "piety" as used here is not applicable to God, for He owes nothing to anyone. On the contrary, all are indebted to Him. And what He does with us is not out of piety, nor is it of debt, nor obligation, but it is out of compassion, mercy, and generosity. For He, being compassionate, merciful, and generous to us in everything, so provides. From this we chiefly ought to recognize that He laid all our sins upon His most precious Son, Jesus Christ our Lord, in order to invest us with the righteousness of the same Jesus Christ our Lord.

WHY DO WE FIND IT MOST DIFFICULT TO TRUST GOD FOR MATERIAL THINGS? (xiv)

In thinking about the difficulties that the human mind has about believing in the truths of Christianity, I have been led further to ask, "What is it that presents the greatest difficulty?" I have come to believe that it is the general acceptance of what comes to us through God's justice that was made upon Christ.

I see this first of all because all men are only alive to their own interests. So they do not involve any self-loss. But those things that most damage their ego will be the most difficult to believe. That is why I now realize that the general pardon of God, which lies at the heart of all the truths of Christianity, is the one that does most damage to our self-dignity. I can argue this from many perspectives, but it will suffice to merely state this from my own experience.

I further find that if I am boldly to divest myself of every external form of justification to enter boldly into the Kingdom of God, then I find that we do not believe that God will equally provide for all the things necessary both for our body and for our soul. It is with the greatest repugnance of mind that we are ready to have unconditional trust in God for both our material and spiritual needs.

But we are constantly asking, "Suppose it is not true that God will provide all that is necessary for my support in spite of my anxiety; what will become of me? Suppose it is not true that God has made such a proclamation of a general assurance of His authority throughout the world; how let down would I be?" It is clear that to the degree someone argues in this way, so he will seek to make provision for himself in one way or the other.

Let me inquire further. Where does a man have greater difficulty in trusting God? Is it in the support of his body or of his soul?

I am forced to believe that we distrust God most of all in terms of our material support. I think this is because man is forced to expect from God more readily what he knows without question he is unable to attain by his own efforts. So he is more likely to distrust

117

himself concerning his justification before God than he is with regard to his bodily needs. So we conclude that a man is forced to depend upon God for his bodily sustenance with much more difficulty than he is for his spiritual needs. It was in thinking about this in my meditations that I came to clearly understand how difficult it is for a rich man to enter into the kingdom of God (Matt. 19:23).

As I long to persuade my mind to depend upon God, both for material as well as spiritual necessities, I recall how Christ promised to give the former to those who seek the Kingdom of God (Matt. 6:33). I also found I must believe that if God provides for me spiritually, He will also provide for me materially. If this argument fails to satisfy me, I have to ask if I am accepted and justified through the proclamation of His general pardon to men.

Since I have entered now into the Kingdom of God, from which the first man was exiled through rebellion, do I not realize that I will never recover the privileges which the first man lost through his rebellion if I also lack faith? Ought I to doubt, then, that God will provide me with material things without my asking? For it is true that the first man, as long as he remained in the Kingdom of God, was provided with material needs without any solicitude on his part. I also realize that among the ways God punished man's rebellion was this: "In the sweat of your brow you will eat your bread" (Gen. 3:19).

SPIRITUAL GIFTS ARE NEVER UNDERSTOOD UNTIL THEY ARE POSSESSED (CX)

Perhaps the highest testimony to the Christian life is this: As the Christian progresses in Christian practice, so does he advance in the Christian distinctives. Indeed the same Christian spirit that led him to progress practically will also lead him to the distinctive views of the faith. So it becomes impossible to determine which comes first, the views or the practice. Both are the consequence of having the Christian spirit within those who accept the Gospel of Christ.

In this realization, the nature of Christianity is not that of a science but of an experience of life. It is one thing therefore to think of faith, hope, and love theoretically, and then to know them in Christian experience, just as it is one thing to know about such natural virtues as kindness, courage, and generosity, and to then actually possess them. So there are people who will approve of soul virtues without actually experiencing them personally.

Likewise, there are many people who approve of faith, hope, and love, but they do not experience them for themselves. No wonder then that they do not experience full satisfaction. Looking at themselves, they live without faith, hope, and love, and are grieved and discontented with life. The more they idealize these virtues, the more they will appear to be unrealizable.

It is only when such virtues are actually experienced that they realize how remote their abstract ideas of them were compared to the reality. So it is with the actual experience of faith, hope, and love. Although they may be saddened and grieved that their full potential is not yet actualized, they take pleasure in the promise of experiencing them more and more. Reflecting upon this I have therefore come to see certain principles.

The first is the certainty that no one can understand the gifts of God except those who actually possess them, that is, those who feel and experience them as an inward reality.

The second is the fact that the inward recognition and feel of them is tested by their satisfaction whenever they hear such Christian topics being discussed. For they will resonate to their truth. Although they only experience them imperfectly, yet they know their reality enough to desire them more and more. For they see how the glory of the Gospel of Christ in God is demonstrated while also revealing the uniformity and weakness of man more and more.

The third is the realization that just as to be kind involves kindness, so for a man to accept the grace of the Gospel involves faith; then he is righteous. To long for the day of judgment involves hope; then he is holy. To love God and one's neighbor involves charity; then he is pious.

The fourth is that a kind person does not lose his character of kindness because of a few lapses of inconsistency. So, too, the Christian does not lose the sense of justification because of some lapses from faith. It is only when he completely neglects the dimension of faith that he is liable to become unjust. And what is true of faith is also true of the one who hopes and the one who loves.

So when I am asked, is it possible for someone to lose the gifts of righteousness, holiness, and piety, the answer is yes if he also loses sight of the faith, hope, and love, for they belong together. So we need to exercise vigilance to guard against this loss. Yet I would see someone as much more secure if he were assured inwardly that he has these gifts than if he merely held on to them outwardly. For it is this sense of security that is itself a gift of God that mortifies and slays sinful lusts, just as its human origin will quicken and excite them. With such confidence, then (not that which comes as it came for the Jews with external, religious scruples, but as characteristic of the Christian virtues of faith, hope, and love), we can say "who shall separate us from the love of Christ?" (Rom. 8:35).

Here I will add that, just as kindness is so intimately connected with a magnanimous nature, so hope and love are so intimately connected with faith. Indeed, one cannot have hope and love without faith. Likewise, it is impossible to be righteous without also being pious and holy. But those who are inexperienced in such Christian realities are also incapable of understanding such truths. This experience alone can be possessed as a gift of God through the benefit of Christ. Only then can they possess faith, hope, and love and therefore be justified, holy, and pious in Christ. Only then will they be intent on apprehending the righteousness, holiness, and piety in which they are already apprehended. They will be like God and His Son Jesus Christ. Amen.

PART II

THE ASSURANCE OF JUSTIFICATION BY FAITH

ON THE BENEFIT OF JESUS CHRIST, CRUCIFIED
BY DON BENEDETTO

*"Since we have acquired one of the most pious and learned works composed
in our times,* Beneficio di Cristi, *it seemed to us that we should publish it for your
comfort and edification, and without the name of the writer, so that you may be moved
more by the content than by the authority of the author."*
—Venice, Bernardo de Bindonis, 1543

CHAPTER 8

THE NATURE OF ORIGINAL SIN

The Holy Scriptures tell us that God created man after His own image and likeness (Gen. 1:26–27). He made man's body free from suffering and his soul righteous, true, good, merciful, and holy. But man was overcome by the desire of knowledge and ate the fruit forbidden by God. He lost the image and likeness of God.

Instead of being like God, man now became like the beasts; indeed even like the very Devil who had abused him. His soul became unrighteous, untrue, cruel, pitiless, and pitted against God. His body became subject to suffering and to a thousand inconveniences and diseases. Not only was he like the beasts, but he was actually inferior to them.

OUR FALLEN INHERITANCE

If our forefathers had obeyed God, they would have left us their righteousness and holiness as our inheritance. But they disobeyed God and left us a heritage of unrighteousness and God's displeasure. It is now impossible for us through our own strength to love God or to align ourselves with His holy will. We are His enemies, and He must punish our sins as a just judge. We can do no more now than wholly trust ourselves upon His holy mercy.

In short, our whole nature has been corrupted by Adam's sin. Previously man had superiority above all creatures; because of the Fall he became an underling to all creaturely things and the bond-slave of Satan, sin, and death. Man has been condemned, therefore, to the miseries of hell. He also lost his judgments completely, calling good evil and evil good. In esteeming false things to be true, he regarded true things to be false.

The psalmist summarizes this by saying that "all men are liars" (Ps. 116:11; cf. Rom. 3:4) and that "there is none that does good" (Ps. 14:3). This is because the Devil, like a stout warrior, rules over the world of which he has become prince and lord. No tongue can express a fraction of our misery as we live in a world clutched by Satan. For we were created by God's own hand; but we have lost the image of God. We have come to behave like the Devil himself, and we are like him also in nature and condition. We will whatever he wills and refuse whatever he dislikes.

We are as a prey to that wicked spirit, and there is no sin so appalling which every one of us would not be ready to do—if the grace of God did not stay us. This is our deprivation of righteousness. It is this forward inclination to all unrighteousness and wickedness that is called "original sin." This is what we brought with us out of our mother's womb, so that we have been born as children of wrath (Eph. 2:3). This original sin had its origin in our first fathers, and this is the cause and fountain of all the sins and iniquities that we commit.

THE NEED FOR RESTORATION

If we are to be delivered from sin and returned to our first innocency, if we are to recover the image of God, then first of all we must learn to realize our own wretchedness. We must see our need.

No man will seek out a doctor unless he knows he is sick. No man will acknowledge the excellency of the physician and how much he is dependent on him unless he knows his own disease to be gripping and deadly. Even so, no man acknowledges Jesus Christ to be the only Physician of our souls unless he first knows his own soul to be sick. Can any person perceive the excellency of Christ or how much he is bound and dependent on Him if he is unaware of his own sinfulness? One must first know of the incurable condition in which he finds himself, the condition we have received through the infection of our first fathers.

CHAPTER 9

THE PURPOSE OF THE LAW

Our God, mindful of His infinite goodness and mercy, sent us His only Son so that the wretched children of Adam might be set free. He knew first of all that it was imperative to make mankind understand its condition of misery. Thus He chose Abraham. In Abraham's seed He promised to bless all the nations (Gen. 12:3). God accepted his offspring as His own peculiar people (Exod. 19:5; Deut. 14:2; Ps. 135:4).

After His people's exodus out of Egypt, out of the bondage of Pharaoh by means of Moses, He gave them the Law. The Law prohibited all lusting and commanded us to love God with all our heart, with all our soul, and with all our strength (Deut. 6:5; Matt. 22:37; Mark 12:30). In this way our whole trust was to rest in Him. We stand ready to give up our lives for His sake, to suffer whatever torture would be given to our bodies, and to surrender up all our property, our dignities, and honors—all for the love of our God. We should be prepared to choose death rather than to do anything that may displease Him whether it be ever so trivial—and do all things with a cheerful heart (1 Cor. 10:31).

Moreover, the Lord commands us to love our neighbor as ourselves (Lev. 19:18; Matt. 22:39; Mark 12:31; Luke 10:27). The meaning of "neighbor" is all manner of men, foes as well as friends (cf. Luke 10:29–37). The story demands that we treat every man as we would want to be treated ourselves; indeed we should love the causes of other men and espouse them as our own.

By looking at this Holy Law in the same way one would gaze in a looking glass, man readily sees his own great imperfection and inability to obey God's commandments. He realizes that he is unable to render to Him the honor and the love which he ought to yield to his Maker.

This, then, is the first purpose of the Law: to make sin known (Rom. 3:20). This the apostle Paul affirms. And in another place he says, "I have not known what sin is but by the Law" (Rom. 7:7).

The second purpose of the Law is to make sin increase. If we, being quite astray from obeying God, become bondslaves to the Devil, we then become full of wicked works and inordinate affections. These cannot abide since God forbids us from lusting. Any increase in such evil works is all the more prohibited (Rom. 7:5, 8). In such manner did the apostle Paul realize how he was a sinner: Sin was dead, but when the Law came, sin rose up again and grew. Thus it has now become much more evident (Rom. 5:19–20).

The third purpose of the Law is to reveal the wrath and judgment of God (Rom. 1:18). For it is the Law that threatened death and everlasting punishment to those who do not keep the Law in every detail. The Holy Scripture says, "Cursed be he that confirms not all the words of the law to do them" (Deut. 27:26; Gal. 3:10). For this reason the apostle Paul says that the Law is a minister of death (2 Cor. 3:7), and that it brings forth wrath (Rom. 4:15). The Law, then, having discovered sin and increased it, shows forth the wrath and indignation of God.

The threat of death reveals the fourth purpose of the Law, which is to make man afraid. Consequently he falls into deep despair and would gladly satisfy the Law. When he clearly sees that he is unable to do so, he also gets angry with God. So he says with all his heart that "there is no God" (Ps. 14:1, 53:1). He says this because he fears being thus punished and chastened by God. As the apostle Paul says, "the wisdom of the flesh is the enemy of God; because it neither is, nor can be, subject to the will of God" (Rom. 8:7).

The fifth purpose of the Law, which is its principal objective and most excellent and necessary office, is to compel a man to go to Jesus Christ (Rom. 10:4). We are reminded of the analogy of the Israelites, who in their dismay were forced to appeal to Moses, saying: "Let not the Lord speak unto us, lest we die; speak you unto us, and we will obey you in all things" (Exod. 20:19; Deut. 5:25–27; 18:16). And the Lord answered "Truly, they have spoken exceedingly well" (Deut. 5:28; Acts 3:22–23). Indeed, they were praised specifically because they asked for a mediator between God and themselves, namely Moses. He was representative of Jesus Christ, the future and true Advocate and Mediator between God and man (Heb. 8:6; 1 Tim. 2:5). With regard to this, God said unto Moses, "I will raise up a prophet among their brethren like unto you, and I will put my word in his mouth; and he shall speak unto them all the things that I shall command him; and I will punish all those that will not obey my word, which he shall speak in my name" (Deut. 18:18–19; cf. Acts 3:22–23).

WHY FORGIVENESS OF SINS DEPENDS UPON JESUS CHRIST

Our God did send the promised great Prophet, His only Son. He did so to free us from the curse of the Law, to reconcile us unto our God, to make our wills conform to His in order to do good works, to heal our self-will, and to restore us to the image of God (Col. 3:10).

Now we know that "there is no other name under heaven given among men, whereby we must be saved" (Acts 4:12). It is only the name of Jesus Christ that saves. So let us run unto Him with the feet of a lively faith and cast ourselves into His arms. For He draws us graciously to Him, saying, "Come unto me, all you who labor and are heavy laden; and I will give you rest" (Matt. 11:28).

HOW CHRIST TAKES US FROM OUR MISERY

What greater comfort or joy can there be in this life compared to this saying in the Gospel of Matthew? When a man feels himself overwhelmed with the intolerable burden of his sins, these words of the Son of God are sweet and precious. He graciously promises to refresh us and to rid us of such great pain.

At the heart of our struggle with sin lies our need to acknowledge our own weakness and misery. This we must do earnestly. For no one can know what is sweet unless he has tasted that which is sour. Therefore, Jesus Christ says, "If any man thirst, let him come to me and drink" (John 7:37). It is as if He meant to say, "If a man does not know himself to be a sinner and has no thirst after righteousness, then he can never taste of the sweetness of Jesus Christ." How sweet it is to talk of Him, to think of Him, and to follow His most holy life.

Having thoroughly realized our own infirmity by means of the Law, let us then listen to John the Baptist. John points us to the Sovereign Physician, saying, "Behold the Lamb of God, which takes away the sin of the world" (John 1:29). For it is Christ who has delivered us from the heavy yoke of the Law (Gal. 3:13). It is He who heals all our infirmities, who reforms our self-will, who returns us to our original innocency, and who restores in us the image of our God. This is just what the apostle Paul speaks of. "Like as by Adam we all are dead, so by Jesus Christ we are all quickened" (1 Cor. 15:22).

It is important that we do not begin to believe that the sin of Adam, which we have inherited from him, should have more part in our lives than the righteousness of Christ, which we have inherited by faith. That would be cause for great complaint, to be conceived and born into sin (Ps. 51:5) and formed by the wickedness of one's parents, which then determines the whole life of a man. But now all such grievance is taken away. For in a similar way, righteousness and everlasting life have come by Jesus Christ. By Him death is now slain (1 Cor. 15:54–57; Hosea 13:14). Concerning this the apostle Paul gives us wonderful discourse:

"Wherefore, as by one man sin entered into the world, and death by sin; and so death passed upon all men, for that all have sinned: for until the law, sin was in the world: but sin is not imputed when there is no law. Nevertheless death reigned from Adam to Moses, even over them that had not sinned after the similitude of Adam's transgression, who is the figure of him that was to come. But not as the offense, so also is the free gift. For if through the offense of one many be dead, much more the grace of God, and the gift by grace, which is by one man, Jesus Christ, has abounded unto many. And not as it was by one that sinned, so is the gift: for the judgment was by one to condemnation, but the free gift is of many offenses unto justification. For if by one man's offense death reigned by one; much more they which receive abundance of grace and of the gift of righteousness shall reign in life by one, Jesus Christ. Therefore as by the offense of one judgment came upon all men to condemnation; even so by the righteousness of one the free gift came upon all men unto justification of life. For as by one man's disobedience many were made sinners, so by the obedience of one shall many be made righteous. Moreover the law entered, that the offense may abound. But where sin abounded, grace did much more abound: That as sin has reigned unto death, even so might grace reign through righteousness unto eternal life by Jesus Christ our Lord" (Rom. 5:12–21).

These words of the apostle Paul clearly demonstrate the truth that we have already discussed: The Law was given to make sin known. Yet we know that sin has no greater power than the power of Christ's own righteousness, which justifies us before God. As Jesus Christ is stronger than Adam, so His righteousness was mightier than the sin of Adam. The sin of Adam was sufficient to make all of us sinners and children of wrath without any misdeed of our own; how much more shall Christ's righteousness be a greater force to make us all righteous and the children of grace without any of our own good works (Rom. 9:8). Indeed, we cannot be righteous unless we ourselves are made good and righteous through faith before we ever do any works.

Someone may despair of God's favor because of some great sin he has done and thinks he will never be forgiven. Let him realize this. It is not that God is not being willing to forgive, or to cover, or to pardon all sins; rather God has already dealt with the matter in the death of His Son, His only begotten, His best beloved. God has now granted a general pardon to all mankind. Everyone who believes the Gospel can enjoy this pardon. This is good news that the apostles have published in all the world. "We beseech you for Jesus Christ's sake, be you reconciled to God; for He that knew no sin was made a sacrifice for our sin, that we might become righteous in Him" (2 Cor. 5:20–21).

The prophet Isaiah foresaw this great goodness of God when he wrote the following beautiful words. These words describe magnificently the passion of our Lord, which could not be better described even in the writings of the apostles.

"Who [he asks] has believed our report? And to whom is the arm of the Lord revealed? For He shall grow up before Him as a tender plant, and as a root out of a dry ground: He has no form nor comeliness; and when we shall see Him, there is no beauty that we should desire Him. He is despised and rejected of men; a man of sorrows, and acquainted with grief: and we hid as it were our faces from Him; He was despised, and we esteemed Him not. Surely, He has borne our griefs, and carried our sorrows: yet we did esteem Him stricken, smitten of God, and afflicted. But He was wounded for our transgressions, He was bruised for our iniquities: the chastisement of our peace was upon Him; and with His stripes we are healed. All we like sheep have gone astray; we have turned every one to his own way; and the Lord has laid on Him the iniquity of us all. He was oppressed, and He was afflicted, yet He opened not His mouth: He is brought as a lamb to the slaughter, and as a sheep before her shearers is dumb, so He opened not His mouth" (Isa. 53:1–7).

THE OFFENSE AND FUTILITY OF SELF-RIGHTEOUSNESS

We who profess to be Christians understand that the Son of God has taken all our sins upon Him, washed them in His own blood, and suffered on the cross for our sakes. How ungrateful and awful for us to still behave, then, as though we could justify ourselves before God. As if we could ever purchase forgiveness by our own works of self-merit.

Who would dare to say that the work of Christ on the cross was insufficient to put away our sins and that we have to add to it in order to be made fully righteous? Yet think about your own ways.

They are completely defiled and tarnished by self-love, self-interest, self-seeking, and a thousand other vanities. Indeed, for these things we need to ask God for further pardon rather than have the nerve to think they could contribute to our salvation!

Let us not forget the warning of the apostle Paul to the Galatians. They were being deceived by false teachers and did not believe that justification by faith was sufficient of itself. They went about with the persistent idea that their own good works could make them righteous. Paul says to them: "Jesus Christ shall profit you nothing, that justify yourselves by the law. For you have fallen from grace. Because we, through the Spirit of faith, wait for the hope of righteousness" (Gal. 5:4–5).

The righteousness of God was revealed upon Mount Sinai with great glory and majesty. What, then, of those who turn their backs upon God's provision for righteousness? What of those who deny Christ's grace in order to justify themselves before God by their own laws and observances? I wish to God they were able to compare the one Law with such substitutes! Then they could judge for themselves.

God is not concerned about giving glory to His own Law. Some, however, believe He would so honor their efforts to keep the Law. But that honor is given singly to His only begotten Son, who alone by His sacrifice has made full amends for all our past, present, and future sins. This is what New Testament writers declare (John 12:32; Heb. 7:27; 9:12, 28; 10:12, 14; 1 John 1:7; 2:2).

As we apply this satisfaction of Jesus Christ to our souls by faith, we enjoy without doubting the forgiveness of sins; we become good and righteous before God through His righteousness. Thus the apostle Paul could say that although he had lived according to "the righteousness which is found in the law," he clearly stated:

"Whatsoever I have gained by it, I have accounted it in all respects to be but loss, for the love of Christ. And especially I esteem all things to be loss for the excellent knowledge of Jesus Christ my Lord; for whom I have counted all things to be loss, and deem them but dung, so that I may win Christ, and be found in Him, not having mine own righteousness which is of the law, but the righteousness which is by the faith of Jesus Christ, which righteousness is given of God, I mean the righteousness of faith, that I may come to the knowledge of Jesus Christ" (Phil. 3:7–10).

These famous words should be engraven upon every Christian's heart. They should ask God to help them really appreciate these statements. The apostle Paul plainly shows that one who truly knows Christ considers all the works of the Law to be harmful. They distract a man from putting his absolute trust in Jesus Christ. He alone is the One upon whom every man ought to depend for his salvation.

The apostle emphasizes this statement about absolute trust all the more by adding that he holds all things as dung so that he might gain Christ and be incorporated into Him. Whoever trusts in his own works, and seeks thereby to justify himself, does not really receive Jesus Christ. Indeed, he is not engrafted into Him.

ONLY GOD CAN JUSTIFY

We need to better understand what Paul means to say about the whole mystery of our faith consisting in this declaration. He helps us by adding and often repeating that he will have nothing to do with all outward justification and all the righteousness that is based upon the keeping of the Law. Instead, he insists that he will clothe himself only with the righteousness that God gives by faith to all who believe their sins are fully dealt with, in Jesus Christ. Paul insists that Jesus Christ "is made our wisdom, righteousness, wholeness, and redemption, to the end (as it is written) that he who will glory, should glory in the Lord, and not his own works" (1 Cor. 1:30–31).

It may be that in the Holy Scriptures there are some passages which, if misunderstood, seem to contradict this holy doctrine of the apostle Paul. As a result, justification and remission of sins are wrongly attributed to works of charity. However, some teachers have shown plainly that those who have understood these Scriptures in the above sense did not really understand them at all.

Therefore, most beloved brethren, let us not follow the popular opinion of the foolish Galatians. Rather, let us follow the truth that the apostle Paul teaches us. Let us give all the glory of justification to God's mercy alone and to the merits of His Son.

It was by the shedding of Christ's blood that we have been set free from the dominion of the Law, the tyranny of sin, and the sting of death (Rom. 7:1). It is He who has brought us into the Kingdom of God to give us life and endless blessing. I further say that He has delivered us from the dominion of the Law since He has given us His Holy Spirit, the Teacher of all truth. He has satisfied the Law to its utmost and given the same satisfaction to all His members, that is, all true Christians. All of us may safely appear at God's throne because we are clothed with the righteousness of Christ.

Thus the Law can no longer accuse us or condemn us. It cannot shake our affections or desires. It cannot increase sin within us. For these reasons the apostle Paul says that the obligation that was against us is canceled by Jesus Christ. He discharged it upon the tree of the cross (Gal. 3:13).

The Law's tyranny has been overcome by Jesus Christ in His resurrection, because death's tyranny has been overcome by the resurrection. Therefore we, as His members, are free to say with the apostle Paul and with the prophet Hosea that death is completely vanquished and destroyed. "O death, where is your sting? O hell, where is your victory? The sting of death is sin, and the strength of sin is the law. But God be praised, who granted us the victory by our Lord Jesus Christ" (1 Cor. 15:55–57; Hosea 13:14).

He is the blessed Seed that has crushed the head of the venomous serpent (Gen. 3:15), the Devil. Thus all those who believe in Jesus Christ can trust His grace to overcome sin, death, and the Devil and hell. He is the blessed Seed of Abraham in whom God has promised blessing to all nations (Gen. 12:3). So everyone should fight against that same horrible serpent that he might be delivered from that curse.

This whole enterprise of evil was so vast that all the forces of the world were unable to prevail against it. Therefore God, the Father of mercy, was moved with compassion because of our miseries. He has given us His only begotten Son, who has delivered us from the venom of the serpent. Christ Himself has become our blessing and righteousness provided we accept Him and renounce all our outward justification.

My dear brethren, let us embrace the righteousness of our Lord Jesus Christ. Let us make His righteousness ours by faith. Let us be assured that we are righteous, not because of our own works, but because of the merits of Jesus Christ. Let us live cheerfully, assured that the righteousness of Jesus Christ has utterly done away with all our unrighteousness. He has made us good, righteous, and holy before God. Beholding us engrafted in His Son by faith, He considers that we are no longer the children of Adam. He considers us His own children. He has also made us heirs of all His riches, joint-heirs with His Son (Rom. 8:17).

CHAPTER 11

THE RESULTS OF A LIVING FAITH IN CHRIST

This holy and living faith is this effective: Whoever believes that Jesus Christ has taken all his sins upon Himself becomes like Christ. He is then able to overcome sin and the Devil; yes, even death and hell.

What is the reason for this change in the believer? The reason is simply that the church—that is to say, every faithful soul—is Christ's bride, and Christ is her Husband. Now we know how the law of marriage operates, namely, the two become one flesh and so become the selfsame being. Then the goods and substance of both are common to both.

WE BENEFIT AS CHRIST'S BRIDE

Just as the dowry of the wife becomes the property of her husband, so likewise the wife speaks of her husband's house and all his wealth as hers. And of course they are. How else could they be one flesh, as the Scripture says?

In the same way, God has married His only begotten and dearly loved Son to the faithful soul; she has nothing else that is her own right save only sin. Yet the Son of God was willing to take her to be His well-beloved spouse. Indeed, He has also taken her peculiar dowry; the dowry of sin.

Jesus Christ says, "The dowry of a man's soul has become mine." That is to say, "All the sins and transgressions of the Law, all God's wrath against man, all the boldness of the Devil over man, all the prison and torture of hell, and all the soul's other evils have become

Mine. They are in My power to do what I want with them. So it is My will to deal with them as I wish.

"Therefore, I blot out the handwriting of ordinances which is against the soul of my wife. I take it out of the way. I fasten it to My cross in Mine own body, and in the same way, I spoil principalities and powers. I make a show of them openly, and triumph over them, consume, and annihilate them utterly" (Col. 2:14–15).

Now when God saw His sinless Son willingly take about Himself the foulness of our iniquity, He made Him to be sin for us; He made Him the very sacrifice for our sin (2 Cor. 5:21). Thus He sharply punished our sin in Him, putting Him to death, even death on the cross. However, as He was His well-beloved and obedient Son, He would not leave Him to death nor suffer His Holy One to see corruption. Instead He raised Christ from death to life, giving Him all power in heaven and earth, and set Him at His right hand in glory (Phil. 2:9; Matt. 28:18).

WE BOAST AS CHRIST'S BRIDE

In response, the bride also says with the greatest joy: "The realms and kingdoms of my most dear Husband and Savior belong to me. By Him I am heir of heaven. My Husband's riches—that is to say His holiness, His innocence, His righteousness, and His Godhead, together with all His virtue and might—are my property. Therefore, in Him I am holy, unblemished, righteous, and godly, and there is not a stain on me. I am shapely and beautiful, because my lawful Husband has no blemish but is stalwart and handsome. Since He is completely mine, all His qualities are consequently mine. Because they are pure and holy, it follows that I have also become pure and holy."

The love and union that are between the soul of a true Christian and the Bridegroom Jesus Christ make all the works of each common to them both. Therefore, when a man says, "Jesus Christ has fasted; Jesus Christ has prayed; Jesus Christ was heard of the Father; Jesus Christ was raised from the dead; Jesus Christ drove devils out of men; Jesus Christ healed the sick, died, rose again, and ascended into heaven"; then a man can likewise say that a Christian has done all these same works. For the works of Christ are the works of the Christian, and He has done them all for the Christian. Indeed, a man can truly say that the Christian has been nailed to the cross, buried, raised again, and has ascended into heaven and been made as a child of God. He is a participant of the divine nature.

WE ACT AS CHRIST'S BRIDE

On the other hand, all the works a Christian does are Christ's works. This is because it is His will to take them as His own. These works are imperfect. He is completely perfect. And so He cannot have anything imperfect before Him. But He has made them perfect through His virtue.

The end of all this is that His bride should always be joyful and well contented; she should not be afraid of anything. There may still be default in her works. Yet she assures herself that the works are acceptable to God in view of His Son, upon whom His eyes are always fastened.

Oh, the immeasurable goodness of God! How greatly is the Christian bound unto God! There is no love of man, no matter how great it may be, that can compare with the love that God bears for the soul of every Christian, of whom Christ is the Bridegroom. The apostle Paul says that Jesus Christ so loved His bride, the church (which is built of living stones, that is, the souls of believing Christians), that He has offered Himself to the death of a cross in order to sanctify her. He has cleansed her with the washing of water by His Word, to join Himself to her, a glorious church, without spot or wrinkle or any such thing. He has cleansed her that she should be holy and unblamable (Eph. 5:25–27). That is to say, He wants her to be presented to Him in holiness and innocence.

As the true and lawful Son of the God who has loved the world so dearly, Jesus Christ Himself says: "He has given His only-begotten

Son, to the intent that everyone who believes in Him should not perish but have life everlasting. For God did not send His Son into the world to condemn the world; but that the world might be saved by Him, so that he that believes in Him shall not be condemned" (John 3:16–17).

HOW CAN I BE ASSURED I BELONG TO CHRIST?

Someone might ask, "What is the manner of this union of holy marriage? How are the soul of the bride and her Bridegroom Jesus Christ united together? What assurance can I have that my soul is united to Jesus Christ and that I have become His spouse? How can I glory in the assurance that I am queen and mistress of His great riches and enjoy these things as a wife enjoys her husband's wealth?

I can readily believe that other folks will receive this honor and glory. But I cannot persuade myself that I am one of those to whom God has given so great a grace."

My dearly beloved brother, I reply to you that your assurance consists in having a true and living faith by which the apostle Peter says God cleanses the hearts of man (Acts 15:9). This faith is grounded in the belief of the Gospel, that belief in the good news which has been published by God throughout the whole world (Luke 2:10). This good news states that God has exercised fully His justice against Jesus Christ, and He has chastened and punished all our sins in Him. Whoever, then, receives the good news and believes it steadfastly has come to the true faith. This soul now enjoys the remission of his sins.

A believer with living faith is reconciled with God. Instead of being a child of wrath, he becomes a child of grace, and he regains the image of God (2 Cor. 3:18). He now enters into God's Kingdom and is indeed made a temple of God (John 3:5; 1 Cor. 3:16). Whoever marries his soul to God's only Son has a faith that is the work of God and that is also the gift of God. The apostle Paul so often reminds us of this (Rom. 5:15, 17; 2 Cor. 9:15; Eph. 2:8).

God gives faith to those whom He calls to Himself in order to justify glorifying them and giving them eternal life. Our Lord Jesus

Christ testifies to this when He says: "This is the will of Him that sent Me, even that everyone who sees the Son and believes in Him should have everlasting life; and I will raise him up again at the last day" (John 6:39).

Again, the Scriptures say: "As Moses lifted up the serpent in the wilderness, so must the Son of man be lifted up; to the end that everyone who believes in Him might not perish, but have life everlasting" (John 3:14–15).

Also He says to Martha, "He that believes in me shall live, although he were dead; and everyone that lives and believes in me, shall not die forever" (John 11:25–26).

And to the crowd of Jews He says: "I came as a light into the world, so everyone who believes in me should not remain in darkness" (John 12:46).

Likewise, in his epistle, the apostle John says: "Herein is the love of God revealed to us; for God is love, and He sent His only-begotten Son into this world, that we might live through Him. And herein is His love known, not that we loved God, but that He loved us, and sent his Son, to make an atonement for our sins" (1 John 4:8–10).

God also sent Him to destroy our enemies. To do this, God made him partaker of our flesh, and of our blood, as the writer to the Hebrews says: "So that through His death He might destroy him that had dominion over death, that is to say the Devil, and free all those who were enslaved throughout their life by the fear of death" (Heb. 2:14–15).

See, then, that we have the testimony of the Holy Scripture for these promises (and for many other promises scattered in various other places), Scriptures we cannot doubt. The Holy Scriptures speak generally, so let no one so distrust himself that he doubts whether they apply to him personally.

It is in this personal assurance that there lies and consists the whole mystery of our holy faith (1 Tim. 3:9; Eph. 3:4–5).

In order that we may better understand it, let us use the illustration of some good and holy king. He proclaims an edict by the sound of the trumpet in all of his realm. The declaration made is that all rebels and all exiles can now safely return home to their families. This is because some dear friend of theirs has made it his cause to pardon them.

Certainly none of these rebels ought to doubt that the king is able to obtain this real pardon on their behalf. Instead everyone should assuredly be able to return home to his house in order to live under the shadow of this good king. However, if someone will not return, then he will certainly bear the consequences. For it is only because of his own unbelief that he will remain at the displeasure of his prince and die in exile.

This good king is the Lord of heaven and earth. It is because of the obedience and merits of our good Brother, Jesus Christ, that we have been pardoned from all our sins. As we said before, He has made an open declaration throughout all the world that we can all return safely into His Kingdom. So whoever believes this proclamation can return immediately into God's realm (out of which we are driven by the offense of our first parents). Such is the Kingdom that is now governed in blessing by God's Holy Spirit.

But whoever disbelieves this proclamation can never enjoy the general pardon that is offered. Instead, for his unbelief he will be doomed to banishment under the tyranny of the Devil, to live and to die in extreme misery, indeed living and dying at the displeasure of the King of heaven and earth.

God's displeasure is just. For we cannot commit a greater offense against the goodness of God than to think of Him as a liar and as a deceiver. Yet in fact we do this whenever we do not believe His promises.

THE CONSEQUENCES OF TRUE FAITH

How awful is this sin of unbelief! For its potency robs God of His glory and perfection. In addition it harms one's soul, torments the mind, and makes one's own conscience miserable.

In contrast, God is glorified by the one who comes to Him with a sincere heart, a certain faith, a belief in His promises, no hesitation, and a firm hold upon all that God has promised him. Such a man will live in sustained peace and joy; he will always praise and thank God. Elected to the glory of eternal life, he knows that he has a secure pledge from his beloved Spouse, the Son of God, whose shed blood has inspired his heart.

Such a holy faith generates a living hope and a constant dependence upon God's mercy toward us. This faith lives and operates in our hearts so that we can rest completely in God and leave all our future to Him. Since we are so confident in God's goodness, we do not fear either the Devil or his servants, nor death itself. The firm and devout trust in God's mercy will expand and exercise our hearts, and direct them godward. This is done with the greatest affection and the most ardent love. That is why the apostle Paul urges us to go in trust before the throne of grace (Heb. 4:16). So he exhorts us not to give up our trust which has the promise of such a great reward (Heb. 10:35). This holy faith never lacks divine love; it is prompted in the heart by the Holy Spirit who is given to us by faith.

Given this faith and power we now are willing and able to endure all sorts of pressures for the love and the glory of our dearest Heavenly Father. Through Christ He has enriched us with an abundance of grace and favor; instead of being enemies, we are adopted as His dear children. When God gives this real faith to man, the power of His love impels him to do good works. Such faith becomes like the choicest fruit trees which yield the sweetest fruits to God and to neighbors.

"Without faith it is impossible to please God" (Heb. 11:6). By faith all the saints of the Old and New Testament were saved (see Heb. 11). The apostle Paul testifies to this in regard to Abraham, of whom the Scripture says: "Abraham believed God and it was imputed to him for righteousness" (Rom. 4:3; cf. Gen. 15:6). Further back he had said, "Therefore, we believe that a man is justified through faith without the works of the law" (Rom. 3:28). Elsewhere

Paul says: "Even so, then, at this present time also there is a remnant according to the election of grace. And if by grace, then it is no more of works: otherwise grace is no more grace. But if it be of works, then it is no more grace" (Rom. 11:5–6).

Paul writes to the Galatians that "No man is justified by the Law in the sight of God, it is evident: for, the 'just shall live by faith' (Hab. 2:4) and the Law is not of faith: but, the man that does them shall live by them" (Gal. 3:11–12; Lev. 18:5). Previously, he had said, "A man is not justified by the works of the Law, but by the faith of Jesus Christ" (Gal. 2:16). Later he also says that if a man can seek to justify himself through the Law, then Christ has died in vain (Gal. 2:21).

In comparing the righteousness of the Law with that of the Gospel, Paul also says to the Romans that the former consists of acts and the latter of faith. "Because if you shall confess with your mouth the Lord Jesus and shall believe in your heart that God has raised Him from the dead, you shall be saved. For with the heart man believes unto righteousness, and with the mouth confession is made unto salvation" (Rom. 10:9–10).

Here you can see, then, how clearly the apostle Paul demonstrates the truth that faith makes a man justified without any help from works.

THE AUTHORITY OF THE FATHERS FOR THE DOCTRINE OF JUSTIFICATION BY FAITH

Augustine

The apostle Paul was followed by the church fathers in confirming and approving this most holy truth of justification by faith. The chief of these is Augustine. In his books *Of Faith and Works*, *Of the Spirit and the Letter*, *Eighty-Three Questions*, and in the letter that he wrote to Pope Boniface, *The Treatise on Psalm 31*, Augustine defends this teaching. He demonstrates that we are justified by faith without the aid of good works. The latter are the effect and not the cause of justification. He also shows that the words of the apostle James, when soundly understood, do not contradict this teaching (see James 2:14–26).

Origen

The same teaching is affirmed by Origen in the fourth book on *The Epistle to the Romans*. He argues that the apostle Paul "means that faith alone is sufficient for justification, so that a man becomes righteous through faith alone, even when he has done no works. In this way, the dying thief is justified without the works of the Law, since the Lord did not look for what he had done in the past, nor did He wait for him to do anything after he believed, but, after He had justified him, upon his confession alone, He accepted him as a companion, just as He was entering into Paradise."

Likewise, the notorious woman referred to in Luke's Gospel, who was at the feet of Jesus Christ, also heard Him say to her, "Your faith has saved you, go in peace" (Luke 7:50).

Origen then adds more to this discussion. "In many places in the Gospel, one sees how the Lord Jesus spoke in such a way to show that faith is a cause of the salvation of believers. Therefore, one is justified through faith, for which the works of the Law are to no avail. On the contrary, where there is no faith—which justified a believer—however much one may do the works commanded by the Law, they can never justify us because they are not built upon the foundation of faith from the start. Although to outward appearances they may look good, yet they can never justify those who do them. They lack the faith which is the true mark of those who are justified by God." Who can glory in his own righteousness, when he hears God saying through the prophet, "All our righteousnesses are as filthy rags" (Isa. 64:6). Accordingly, we can only justly glory, not in ourselves, but in the faith of the Cross of Christ (Origen's commentary on *The Epistle to the Romans*, Book 3:9).

Basil

In his homily on humility, Basil specifically declares that the Christian can only consider himself justified through faith in Christ. These are his own words: "The Apostle says, let him who glories, glory in the Lord, saying that 'God made Christ to be our wisdom, righteousness, sanctification, and redemption, so that as it is written, let him who glories, glory in the Lord'" (1 Cor. 1:30–31; cf. Jer. 9:23–24).

This means the only exercise of glory that man can achieve authentically is to glory in the Lord. In this way he recognizes true righteousness, and he is only justified by faith in Jesus Christ. The apostle Paul glories in despising his own righteousness, in seeking through faith, and in the righteousness of Christ that comes from God (*Homily on Humility*, 20:3).

Hilary

Hilary says, "The scribes, seeing Jesus Christ only as a man, were upset that a man should claim he could forgive sins, and give pardon, a thing even the Law could not do, because faith alone justifies" (*Commentary on Matthew's Gospel*, 8:6).

Ambrose

Ambrose expounds on the following words of the apostle Paul: "Whoever believes on him that justifies the ungodly, his faith is counted for righteousness. Even as David also describes the blessedness of man unto whom God imputes righteousness without works" (Rom. 4:5–6).

He comments on this as follows: "The apostle Paul says that whoever believes in Christ, that is the Gentile, has his faith accounted for righteousness' sake, as Abraham did. How then did the Jews think that they could justify themselves through the works of the Law, and also justify themselves as Abraham was, when Abraham was justified not by works but only through faith? Therefore the Law is not necessary, for the sinner is justified before God through faith alone, according to the purpose of God's grace. As Paul says, God has willed that with the end of the Law, the unrighteous can only ask for faith in the grace of God for his salvation. David agreed. The Apostle quotes what David said as an instance of this: 'Blessed is he whose transgression is forgiven, whose sin is covered. Blessed is the man unto whom the Lord imputes not iniquity, and in whose spirit there is no guile' (Ps. 32:1–2). David means that those who are blessed are those whom God has willed to justify in his sight by faith alone. This is without effort or observance, and so he preaches the blessedness of the time in which Christ will be born. As the Lord Himself says, 'Many prophets and kings have desired to see those things which you have seen and have not seen them; to hear those things which you hear and have not heard them'" (Luke 10:24).

Ambrose also expounds in his beginning chapter of *The First Epistle to the Corinthians* that whoever believes in Christ is justified without works and without any merit. This believer receives the forgiveness of his sins through faith alone (Commentary on *The First Epistle to the Corinthians*, 1:4).

He also makes the same point in a letter to Irenaeus: "No one can glory in his works, because no one is justified by his works. He who is righteous has righteousness as a gift, because he is made righteous by Jesus Christ." So it is faith that delivers through the blood of Christ. Blessed then is he whose sin is forgiven and pardoned. (*Epistle to Irenaeus* 30, 113:11, 73).

Bernard of Clairvaux

Bernard of Clairvaux in his sixty-seventh sermon on the Song of Songs also confirms the truth of justification by faith, saying that our merits have no value at all in making us righteous. Rather he attributes it entirely to grace that freely makes us justified. Only in this way are we freed from the bondage of sin. He adds that Jesus Christ marries the soul, linking the soul to Himself through faith without any merit on our part (*On the Song of Songs* 67:11).

To avoid being too lengthy in citing these authorities, let me conclude with a beautiful instruction given by Ambrose in his book called *Of Jacob and the Blessed Life*. This saintly man notes that Jacob was not the firstborn by birth. So Jacob hid himself under his brother's clothes, adorned himself with Esau's garments and aromas, and thus disguised himself as another person. He then presented himself to his father, to receive the blessing for his own benefit (Gen. 27).

Likewise, we need to clothe ourselves under the precious perfection of our Elder Brother and Savior if we want to be accepted as righteous in the presence of God (*Of Jacob and the Blessed Life*, 11, 11:9). This is certainly true, for if we appear before God without being clothed in the righteousness of Christ, we will certainly be condemned as unjust and worthy of every divine punishment. If, on the other hand, God sees us clothed with the righteousness of Christ, He will surely accept us as just and holy and worthy of eternal life.

Thus those who pretend that they can achieve justification by keeping the commandments of God (which comprise loving God with all one's heart, soul, strength, and one's neighbor as one's self, Matt. 22:37–39, Mark 12:30–31, Luke 10:27) are certainly very rash. Who could be so arrogant and so foolish that he permits himself to believe that he has entirely kept these two precepts? How can he not see that the Law of God requires a perfect spiritual love from man, and therefore it condemns every imperfection! So let such a one reflect upon his actions which may seem all right to himself. Then he will find that such actions should be called transgressions of that Holy Law, since they are completely impure and imperfect.

How then do the words of the psalmist David ring out: "Enter not into judgment with your servant; for in your sight shall no man living be justified" (Ps. 143:2). Again Solomon asks: "Who can say, my heart is clean?" (Prov. 20:9).

Job exclaims, "What is man that he should be clean? And he that is born of woman, that he should be righteous? Behold, he puts no trust in his saints. Yea, the heavens are not clean in his sight. How much more abominable and filthy is man, who drinks iniquity like water" (Job 15:14–16). John also says, "If we say we are without sin, we deceive ourselves" (1 John 1:8). Likewise the Lord taught us that every time we pray, we should say: "Forgive us our trespasses, as we forgive those who trespass against us" (Matt. 6:12).

From these references we can see how foolish are those who depend on their own self-righteousness and presume that they can make use of their works to save themselves as well as their neighbor.

As though our Lord Jesus Christ had not already said to them, "When you shall have done all those things which are commanded to you, say, 'We are unprofitable servants. We have done that which was our duty to do'" (Luke 17:10).

So you see, even if we have performed God's law to the full, we should still think of ourselves as unprofitable servants. Now since all are so remotely distant from even such a perfect ordinance, how dare anyone glory in himself? Or how dare anyone think that he has accumulated so much merit, that there is an overplus, to give us credit for others? [This is a possible reference to the masses that were offered for the dead and the granting of indulgences to souls in purgatory.]

OUR RIGHTEOUSNESS IS IMPUTED ONLY BY CHRIST

Let the proud sinner who thinks he has done praiseworthy things before the eyes of the world take note. Does he really think he can pretend also to justify himself in God's eyes? Does he not realize that all works that come from impure motives and unclean hearts are also impure and unclean? Consequently they can never be either pleasing to God nor efficacious for a sinner's justification. We must first purify our hearts if we want to have such works be pleasing to God. Such purification consists of faith. The Holy Spirit affirms this in the words of the apostle Peter (Acts 15:9).

Thus we cannot say that the unjust and sinful man can become righteous before God through his own works. Rather we must say that faith cleanses our hearts from all sin and makes us good, righteous, and pleasing to God. As a result our ensuing works, although defective and imperfect, are also pleasing to God, because we have become children of God through faith.

God regards our works as a merciful Father and not as a stern judge. He has compassion upon our weakness, but He looks on us as members of His first-born Son, whose righteousness and perfection are the substitute for our own uncleanness and imperfection. These imperfections are not imputed to us, and they do not come under God's judgment, because they are hidden under Christ's purity and innocence.

But what can a man do to merit such a great gift and treasure as Christ Himself? It is a treasure given only through the grace, favor, and mercy of God. It is faith alone that receives such a gift and permits us to enjoy the forgiveness of sin. Therefore, when the apostle Paul and the church fathers say that faith alone justifies without works, they mean that faith alone enables us to enjoy general pardon and to receive Christ into our hearts by faith (Eph. 3:17).

Christ has given peace to our consciences and satisfied divine judgment for our sins. He has quenched the fire of hell and the wrath of God against us. If it were not for this, our natural corruption and acquired depravity would have hurled us into the abyss.

Christ has destroyed the devils with all their power and tyranny. Not all the achievements of mankind could ever accomplish this. For such power and glory is reserved for the Son of God alone. Our blessed Christ has power above all others, on earth and in heaven (Matt. 28:18). In spite of all His merits, He gives Himself to those who despair of themselves and place their entire hope of salvation upon Him and His merits.

THE CHARACTER OF JUSTIFIED FAITH

Let no one be deceived when he hears that faith alone justifies. No one should reduce it to "cheap grace" as do pseudo-Christians who drag everything down to their own worldly level. For them, true faith consists in believing in the story of Jesus Christ in the same way in which they might believe about Caesar and Alexandra. This kind of belief is credence in history, and it is based on the merely factual writings of man. It is superficially accepted mentally as custom may dictate. It is like the faith of the Turks who believe in the myth of the Koran for the same reason.

Belief such as this is mere fantasy. It does not renew a man's heart at all nor can it warm the heart with divine love. No good works, nor new life, will follow from it. So they falsely argue that faith alone does not justify, but deeds are also needed. This is contrary to the Holy Scriptures and to the Father of the church.

My reply concerning this historical belief is that it is so futile when works are added to it, that it not only does not justify, but it will cast people into hell itself. For such people are like the foolish virgins who had no oil in their lamps (Matt. 25:3). That is to say, they were those who had no living faith in their hearts.

The faith that makes men righteous is a work of God; through it our old man is crucified (Rom. 6:6). And we are all transformed through Jesus Christ. Thus we become new creatures and are dearly beloved children of God. It is this divine faith that grafts us into the death and resurrection of Jesus Christ. Consequently, it modifies our flesh with all its affections and lusts.

We realize that through the efficacy of grace, we have died with Christ. We detach ourselves from this world as well as from ourselves. And we realize that those who died in Christ should mortify their earthly members. That is to say, we should mortify the vicious affections of the mind and the carnal appetites (Col. 3:5–8). Now that we know that we have risen with Christ, we need to live a holy and spiritual life. We need a life like that which we shall live in heaven itself after there is a general resurrection.

This holy faith enables us to enjoy the general pardon that is proclaimed by the Gospel. Introducing us to God's Kingdom, it pacifies our consciences and maintains us in perpetual joy that is spiritual and holy. This same faith unites us with God and makes Him dwell in our hearts. It clothes our souls with Himself, and consequently His Holy Spirit moves us to share the same things that Christ had while He lived among men: humility, meekness, obedience to God, charity, and all the other perfections through which we may regain the image of God. Christ rightly attributes blessing to this inspired faith which cannot exist without good works and holiness.

How is it, then, that a Christian is not holy, if Christ has become his sanctification through faith? Because of faith, we are justified and holy. For this reason the apostle Paul almost invariably called saints those whom we called Christians (Rom. 1:7; 15:25; 1 Cor. 14:33; Eph. 1:1; Col. 1:2). If they do not have the Spirit of Christ then they do not belong to Christ; they are not Christians. But if they have the Spirit of Jesus Christ to rule over and govern them, then we cannot doubt that although justified by faith, they will not become lazy about doing good works. For the Spirit of Christ is the Spirit of love. And love cannot be idle or afraid of doing good deeds.

Indeed, if we want to tell the truth, man can never do good works unless he knows that he has been made righteous through faith from the start. Before this he has done the works for his own self-justification rather than for the love and glory of God. So he spoils them by self-love and self-interest.

But the man who knows that he is justified by faith through the merits and righteousness of Christ works solely for the love of God and Christ His Son. He does not do so for any self-love or self-justification. The result is that the true Christian (that is, one who sees himself justified by the righteousness of Christ) does not ask himself whether good works are demanded or not. Instead he is compelled and impelled by the power of divine love. He offers himself willingly to do all the good works that are holy and Christlike. He will never cease to do well.

However, he who never experienced the marvelous effects of faith described above and who never has had such faith to inspire his heart as a Christian may realize that he still does not have Christian faith. Let him then pray earnestly that God might give him this faith: "Lord, help mine unbelief" (Mark 9:24). When he hears it said that only faith makes a man righteous, do not let him deceive himself and ask, "Why should I weary myself in doing good works? Is faith not enough to send me to heaven?"

To such a one my answer is that it is only faith that sends us to heaven. But take good heed, for "the devils do also believe and tremble," as the apostle James says (James 2:19). O miserable man! Do you really want to go to heaven with your sins? By this false conclusion you will know, my brother, how you err. For you pretend to have a faith that makes men righteous, and you really do not have it. "You say that you are rich, and have no need of anything; and you do not see how poor you are, wretched, blind, and naked. I counsel you to buy of me gold tried in the fire, that you may be rich; and white raiment that you may be clothed, and that the shame of your nakedness do not appear; and anoint your eyes with eyesalve, that you may see" (Rev. 3:17–18).

This is justifying faith. It is like a flame of fire which only bursts forth in its brightness. It is like the flame that burns the wood without the help of light; yet the flame cannot be without the light. In similar fashion it is true that faith alone consumes and burns away sin without the help of works, and yet that same faith cannot be without good works. Therefore, as we see a flame of fire that gives no light, we know by such an illustration that it is vain and deceptive. Even so, when we do not see some light of good works in a man, it is an evidence that he does not have the true and inspired faith that God gives to justify and to glorify His elect.

Know that it is really true what the apostle James meant when he said: "Show me your faith by your words; and I will show you my faith by my works" (James 2:18). His meaning was that he who is absorbed in ambition and worldly pleasures does not truly believe, even though he says he does. He does not show within himself the effects of faith.

Also we may compare this most holy justifying faith to the divinity which was in Jesus Christ on earth. For He was true man but without sin. He did wonderful things, healed the sick, gave sight to the blind, walked upon the water, and raised up the dead. Yet these marvelous works did not make Christ become God. Before He did any of these things He was God, the legitimate and only begotten Son of God. So He did not need to work such miracles in order to make Himself God. But as He was God, therefore He did them. Thus the miracles that Christ wrought did not make Him become God, but rather showed clearly that He was God.

So it is with true faith. There is a divinity within the soul of the Christian which is never weary of well doing. It is not necessary to do these works to become a Christian. (That is, to be righteous, good, holy, and acceptable to God in Himself.) But he does them because he is already a Christian by faith. This does not make the Christian righteous and good in himself, but rather it already shows him to be good, righteous, and holy in Christ. So then, just as Christ's divinity was the cause of His miracles, even so justifying faith, as it works through love, is the motive of the good works that a Christian does.

THE CHARACTER OF CHRIST'S FAITH IN THE BELIEVER

A man may say that Jesus Christ did this or that miracle. Not only did they glorify God, but they were also a great honor to Jesus Christ as a man. For in His obedience, even unto death, He was vindicated by God's power in His resurrection.

Faith works in the Christian similarly, for through the union of faith with the believer, what belongs to one is attributed to the other. Thus good works are the fruits and testimonies of a living faith. They proceed from it just as light proceeds from a flame as I have said before. It is by this holy faith which embraces Jesus Christ that our soul is also joined with Christ. It is so united and knit to Him, that whatever merit Christ has, the same is imputed to the soul. It is as if the soul had merited and deserved it. Therefore, says Augustine: "God crowns His own gifts in us."

Jesus Christ bears good witness of this union of the soul with Him when He prays to His Father for His apostles and for those who believe in Him by their preaching: "I pray not [He says] for them only, but also for those that shall believe in me through their word, to the end that they may be all one; that, like as Thou my Father art in me and I in Thee, so they also may be one in us, that the world

154

may believe that Thou has sent me and that I have given them the glory which Thou has given me, so as they should be one, like as Thou and I are one" (John 17:20–22).

Likewise it appears that we believe the word of the apostles who preach that Jesus Christ "died for our sins, and rose again for our justification" (Rom. 4:25). We all become one with Him. And as He is all one with God, we also become all one with God by means of Jesus Christ (1 Cor. 6:17). What a wonderful glory this is for the Christian!

To him it is granted, through faith, this possession of unspeakable benefits which the angels long to behold! (1 Peter 1:12).

THE DIFFERENCE BETWEEN TRUE FAITH AND SELF-RIGHTEOUSNESS

From this discourse we may plainly see the difference between our position and that of those who defend justification by faith and works together. We do agree with them in establishing the necessity for works, for we affirm that faith which justifies cannot be without good works. This is evident in those who are righteous and do good works (1 Peter 2:12).

But we differ from them in this respect: We insist that faith makes men righteous without the help of works. The reason is that by faith "We put on Christ" (Gal. 3:26–27) and make His holiness and righteousness to be our own. Since Christ's righteousness is given to us by faith, we cannot be so thankless, blind, and impious as not to believe that He is sufficient in ability to make us acceptable and right before God. We may conclude this with the Apostle's words: "If the blood of bulls and oxen, and the ashes of a heifer sprinkling the unclean, sanctifies to the purifying of the flesh: how much more shall the blood of Christ, who through the eternal Spirit offered Himself without spot to God, purge your conscience from dead works to serve the living God?" (Heb. 9:13–14).

So let the devout Christian decide which of these two options is the true, holy, and worthy one to be preached. Is it ours, which advances the benefit of Jesus Christ and humbles the pride of man, or is it that which exalts a man's own works against Christ's glory? For he who affirms faith in himself does not justify; rather he defaces the glory and the benefit of Jesus Christ. This puffs up the pride of man, which cannot bear to be justified freely by our Lord Jesus Christ without some merit of his own.

Some argue that it is a great incentive to do good works by saying that a man makes himself righteous before God by means of them. I confess that good works are acceptable to God and that He of His grace and liberality rewards them to heaven. But we also add along with Augustine that no works are good except those done by the persons that become righteous through faith. For if the tree is not good, it cannot yield good fruit.

We also say that those who become righteous through faith, those who depend only on God's righteousness that has been purchased by Christ, will make no bargains with God about their works. They are not tempted to believe they can buy their justification. Being inflamed with the love of God and a desire to glorify Jesus Christ, they will make every effort to do God's will.

They will fight vigorously against the love of self, the world, and the Devil. When they fall through the weakness of the flesh, they rise again even more anxious to do good, for so much more have they become enamored with God. Since they know He does not impute sins to them, they become more deeply united to Christ. For it is He who has made full amends for all His members upon the tree of His cross, and who continues to make intercession for them before the Eternal Father. Because of His love for His only begotten Son, God always looks upon them with a gentle countenance; He governs and defends them as His most dear children. At the end He will give them the inheritance of the world and will make them conform to the glorious image of Christ (Rom. 8:29).

It is these loving thoughts that spur on the true Christians to do good works. When they consider that they have become children of God and partakers of His divine nature through faith, they are moved by the Holy Ghost dwelling within them to live as it becomes the children of such a great Lord. So they are greatly ashamed when they do not maintain the decorum of their heavenly nobility.

Therefore, Christians will make every effort to imitate their first-born Brother, Jesus Christ. They will live in the greatest humility and meekness and in all things seek the glory of God. They give their lives for their brethren, do good to their enemies, and glory in the sufferance of reproaches and in the cross of our Lord Jesus Christ (Gal. 6:14). They say with Zacharias: "We being delivered out of the hands of our enemy are to serve God without fear, in holiness and righteousness, all the days of our life" (Luke 1:74–75).

Christians say also with the apostle Paul: "The grace of God that brings salvation has appeared to all men, teaching us that denying ungodliness and worldly lusts, we shall live soberly, righteously, and godly in this present world; looking for that blessed hope, and the glorious appearing of the great God and our Savior Jesus Christ" (Titus 2:11–13).

These and similar thoughts, desires, and affections are prompted by inspired faith in the minds of the justified. If there is one who does not feel these divine affections and operations in his heart, either in whole or in part, but is given over to the flesh and the world, let him realize that he has not yet justifying faith. Indeed he is not a member of Christ. Because he does not have Christ's Spirit, he is continuously none of His. He that does not belong to Christ is not a Christian (Rom. 8:9). So let human prudence cease from now on to fight against the righteousness of the most holy faith. Let us all give the glory of our justification to the merits of Jesus Christ in whom we are clothed through faith (Gal. 3:26–27).

CHAPTER 12

HOW THE CHRISTIAN CLOTHES HIMSELF WITH JESUS CHRIST

I have said thus far what seems simple and clear enough to a Christian who clothes himself with Jesus Christ. Yet I intend to say more about this true knowledge. For the good and faithful Christian will never see it as tedious or troublesome, even if it were repeated a thousand times.

Therefore I say that the Christian who knows Jesus Christ knows all His righteousness, holiness, and innocence as his own through faith. And just as a man who presents himself to some great lord or prince makes every effort to appear handsomely dressed, the Christian in the same way desires to be clothed and attired with the perfection of Christ in all His purity before he presents himself boldly before God, the Lord of all. He will be confident that through Christ's merits, he is in good standing; it is as if he had purchased all that Christ has purchased and deserved. Indeed, then, faith certainly makes every one of us possess Christ and all that belongs to Him. We own Christ and His riches in the same way that each of us possesses our own clothing.

Therefore to be clothed with Jesus Christ is nothing else but to believe in all certainty that Christ is wholly ours. Indeed, and so He is, if we believe Him and hold on to the reality that this heavenly garment makes us acceptable and pleasing to God (cf. Matt. 22:1–12).

For it is most certain that He, as our dearest Father, has given us His Son. This means that all the Son's righteousness and all that He is, can, or ever will be, shall be in our possession and jurisdiction. As a consequence, we can lawfully glory in them.

Thus the Christian must have a steadfast faith and firm belief that all the goods, graces, and riches of Christ are his own. For since God has given them to us in Christ, how could it be that He would not give us all things with Him? (Rom. 8:32). If this is true, as indeed it is, then the Christian can rightly say, "I am the child of God; and Jesus Christ is my brother. I am master of heaven and earth, of hell and of death, and of the Law itself. For the Law cannot accuse me, neither can it curse me, because the righteousness of God has become mine in Christ."

It is this faith alone that enables a man to be called a Christian. It is this which clothes him with Jesus Christ. Properly, then, this may be called a great mystery (1 Tim. 3:9), a mystery that contains marvelous and undeclared things that concern the greatness of God. Such marvels cannot enter into a man's heart unless God softens it with His holy grace (1 Cor. 2:9–10). But this He has promised to do as He says in Ezekiel the prophet: "A new heart also will I give you, and a new spirit will I put within you. And I will take away the stony heart out of your flesh, and I will give you a heart of flesh" (Ezek. 36:26).

Without this belief that everything he has depends upon Jesus Christ, he cannot call himself a true Christian. Nor can he ever have a quiet and joyful conscience. Nor can he have a good and clear mind that is willing to act decisively. Instead he will easily fall away from good works. Or rather he will never be able to do good works that are truly righteous. For righteousness comes only by the belief and trust that we have in the merits of Jesus Christ. It is this alone that makes men true Christians and strengthened, hopeful, and happy lovers of God. Only such are able to do good works, for they are possessors of God's Kingdom and of God Himself. Only such are His own dearly beloved children in whom the Holy Ghost does truly dwell.

What mind is so abject, cold, and vile that the inestimable grandeur of the gift He has bestowed does not inspire such a one to become like Him in good works? For Christ was also given to us by the Father to be an example. We must therefore look continually at Him and define our whole life as a true image of the life of Jesus Christ. For as much as Christ, says the apostle Peter, "suffered for us, leaving us an example, that we should follow in His footsteps" (1 Peter 2:21).

CLOTHED WITH THE EXAMPLE OF CHRIST

It is from this consideration that there arises another way of clothing a man's self with Christ. This we may term "pattern-clothing." For as the Christian must regulate his whole life by the example of Christ, so he must also fashion himself like Him in all his thoughts, words, and deeds (cf. Eph. 4:22–24). He must leave his former bad life in the past and clothe himself with this new life, namely, with the life of Christ. It is because of this that the apostle Paul says: "Let us therefore cast off the works of darkness, and let us put on the armor of light; let us walk honestly as in the day, not in feasting nor in drunkenness, not in clambering and wantonness, not in strife and iniquity, but put on the Lord Jesus Christ, and make not provision for the flesh, to fulfill the lusts thereof" (Rom. 13:12–14).

It is in reflection upon this that the true Christian, the one who loves Jesus Christ, speaks like this to himself: "In spite of the fact that Jesus Christ has no need for me, He went ahead and redeemed me with His own blood. He became poor to enrich me. Therefore, I will give away my goods, yes and even my very life, for the love and welfare of my neighbor. And as I am clothed with Jesus Christ by the love that He has shown to me, so I will do the same for my neighbor in Christ." Whoever does not follow this pattern is no true Christian. For he cannot say that he loves Christ if he does not also love the members and brothers of His family.

If we do not love our neighbor for whose sake Christ shed His blood, we cannot truly say that we love Jesus Christ. For He, being equal with God, was obedient to His Father even to the death of the cross (Phil. 2:6, 8). He has loved and redeemed us, giving Himself for us with all that He ever had. In the same way, we who are rich and have abundance of good things at Christ's hand must also in obedience to God offer and give our works and all that we have. Yea, we must give our very selves to our neighbors and brethren in Jesus Christ. We must serve them and help them in their need, and be to them as another Christ.

Then as Jesus Christ was lowly and gentle, and removed from all strife and debate, so we must set our whole mind upon being holy and meek. We must avoid all strife and impatience in words as well as argument, and do so literally (2 Tim. 2:23). For as Christ endured all persecutions and disorders of the world for the glory of God, so we should patiently and cheerfully bear the persecutions and reproaches which false Christians impose on those who would live godly lives (2 Tim. 3:12). This will come to all who will live faithfully in Jesus Christ. Christ gave His life for His enemies and prayed for them upon the cross (Luke 23:34). So we should also pray for our enemies and willingly spend our lives for their welfare.

This is what it means, according to the apostle Peter, to follow Christ's footsteps. For when we recognize that Christ with all His riches belongs to us, and that we are clothed with Christ and become pure and free from all stains, then there remains nothing more for us to do but to glorify God by imitating Christ. All else we can accomplish is to do to our brethren what Christ has done for us. This is warranted by His word that, whatever we do to His brethren and ours, He accepts it as a benefit that is done for Him (Matt. 10:42; Mark 9:41).

Since true Christians are members of Christ, we can certainly neither do good nor evil to true Christians without doing the same to Christ. For He rejoices or suffers in His own members. Therefore, just as Christ is our garment by faith, so we also ought to be a garment of love to our brothers. We should take good care of them as we do of ourselves. They are members of our body, of whom Christ is the Head. This, then, is the godly love and charity that springs and proceeds from true and unfeigned faith, which God has breathed into His elect. It is the faith that the apostle Paul writes about, as "working by love" (Gal. 5:6).

However, the life of our Lord Jesus Christ was a perpetual cross, full of troubles, reproaches, and persecutions. So we continually carry His cross if we would be like Him (2 Tim. 2:11–12; Gal. 6:14). As Christ said: "If any man will come after me, let him deny himself, and take up His cross daily and follow me" (Luke 9:23).

CLOTHED WITH THE AFFLICTIONS OF CHRIST

The chief reason for this cross is that by it, our God intends to mortify the affections of our mind and the lusts of our flesh. The end result is that we may see in ourselves the grand perfection, that we have embraced our Lord Jesus Christ by being grafted into Him (John 15:5). It is also His will that our faith, which is refined like gold in the furnace of troubles, should shine brightly to His glory (1 Peter 1:7). It is also His intent that His great power should shine through our infirmities which the world cannot help seeing in us. Our frailty becomes strengthened by troubles and persecutions; the more it is beaten down and oppressed, the more it is strong and steadfast (2 Cor. 12:9–10). The apostle Paul says: "We have this treasure in earthen vessels, that the excellency of the power may be of God and not of us. We are troubled on every side, yet not distressed; we are perplexed but not in despair; persecuted but not forsaken; cast down, but not destroyed; always bearing about in the body the dying of the Lord Jesus, that the life of Jesus might be made manifest in our mortal flesh" (2 Cor. 4:7–10).

Seeing that our Lord Jesus Christ and all His dear disciples glorify God by tribulations, let us also embrace them joyfully. Let us say with the apostle Paul: "God forbid that I should glory, save in the cross of our Lord Jesus Christ" (Gal. 6:14).

Let us so deal with the world that whether it understands the truth or not, it may see the wonderful effects that God works in those who sincerely embrace the grace of His Gospel. I repeat, let us so behave before worldlings that they may see how calmly true Christians can endure the loss of all their goods, the death of their children, slanders, diseases of the body, and the persecutions of false Christians.

Let the world see how only true Christians can worship God in spirit and in truth (John 4:23). Let them see how only true Christians hold on to whatever is good, righteous, and holy, praising Him always for the same, whether it be in prosperity or in adversity. Let them see how the true Christian thanks Him as one would thank a most gracious and loving Father; at the same time he acknowledges it to be a great and true gift of God's goodness to suffer any adversity. And let all this chiefly be for the sake of the Gospel and for the sake of following the steps of Christ.

Especially let the world know that "Tribulation works patience, and patience trial, and trial hope, and hope makes us not ashamed" (Rom. 5:3–5, cf. James 1:3–4).

I repeat, patience engenders trial. While God has promised help in trouble to such as trust in Him, we find by experience that we will continue strong and always steadfast as we are upheld by the hand of God. This is something that we could not do on our own without all the powers that we now have at our disposal. So then it is by patience that we find our Lord gives us the help that He has promised for our need; and so He confirms our hope.

It would be a gross ingratitude not to believe that such help and favor is also available for the future. For in the past we have found these helps to be so certain and constant, indeed, right up to the present. Why do we have to say any more? It should suffice us to know that true Christians are through tribulation clothed with the image of Christ crucified. If we bear this willingly, with a good heart, we shall finally be clothed with the image of Christ glorified (Rom. 8:17). "For, as the passions of Jesus Christ do abound, so through Him shall the consolations super-abound" (2 Cor. 1:5). For, if we suffer with Him here below for a time, we shall also reign with Him there above forever (Rom. 8:17).

CHAPTER 13

SOME REMEDIES FOR THE LACK OF ASSURANCE

Since the Devil and man's wisdom constantly try to deprive us of this most holy faith, it is very needful for the Christian to have his weapons always in readiness to defend himself. For such mischievous temptation seeks to deprive the soul of its life. Among the weapons that are mightiest and best there are four. These are prayer, the remembrance of holy baptism, the frequent use of the Holy Communion, and meditation upon the reality of our predestination.

PRAYER

In the exercise of prayer we may well say with the father of the demented boy, "Lord Jesus, help my unbelief" (Mark 9:24). Likewise we may say with the apostle, "Lord, increase our faith" (Luke 17:5). If we are dominated by the continual desire to grow in faith, hope, and love, then we will "pray continually" (1 Thess. 5:17) as the apostle Paul instructs us. For prayer is nothing else but a fervent mind that is settled upon God.

BAPTISM

By the remembrance of baptism we become more certain that we are at peace with God. And as the Apostle Peter indicates, the ark of Noah was a figure of baptism. For just as Noah was saved from the Flood by the ark because he believed in the promises of God, so also are we saved by faith in baptism from God's wrath (1 Peter 3:20–21). Such a faith is founded upon the Word of Christ, who says,

"Whoever believes and is baptized shall be saved" (Mark 16:16). This is very reasonable because in baptism we "put on Jesus Christ" (Gal. 3:27).

When we put on Christ in baptism, we are made partakers of His righteousness and benefit from His merits. Under this precious garment, our sins, which we commit in our weakness, are hidden, and they are not imputed to us. Thus the apostle Paul says that the blessing of the Psalmist also belongs to us, namely: "Blessed are they, whose transgressions are forgiven, and whose sins are covered. Blessed is the man to whom the Lord imputes not iniquity" (Rom. 4:7–8; Ps. 32:1–2).

But it is necessary for the Christian to guard against taking these words as an excuse to license sin. For this false doctrine does not apply to those who honor themselves with the name of Christian. It is characteristic only of those who confess merely with their mouths and yet deny Him with their deeds. This verse concerns only true Christians who, although they fight manfully against the flesh, the world, and the Devil, still fall daily, and are constrained to say: "Lord forgive us our debts" (Matt. 6:12). It concerns only the true Christians, to comfort and encourage them knowing that He is also our Advocate as well as the atonement for His members.

Therefore, when we are tempted to doubt the forgiveness of our sins, and our conscience begins to trouble us, then we must equip ourselves with true faith. Then we have recourse to the precious blood of Jesus Christ, shed for us upon the altar of the Cross.

HOLY COMMUNION

Under the veil of a most holy sacrament, Christ distributed to His disciples at the last supper the reality that we should celebrate the remembrance of His death. For it is by that same visible sacrament that our troubled consciences can be assured of our atonement with God. The blessed Jesus Christ made His covenant with us when He said: "This is my body which is given for you" (Luke 22:19). Again

He promised forgiveness when He said, "This is my blood of the new testament, which is shed for many" (Mark 14:24).

We know that "a testament," says the apostle Paul, "even be it made by man, yet nevertheless if it be authenticated, no one can undervalue it or add anything to it" (Gal. 3:15). And the new testament cannot be enforced until the testator is dead. Only then has it full power, after the party's decease. Thus did Christ make His testament, in which He has promised us the forgiveness of sins, the grace and favor of His relationship with His Father, and mercy unto everlasting life. But in order that the said testament could be in full force, He confirmed it with His own precious blood, and therefore with His own death. Because of this, the Apostle says that Jesus Christ is "The Mediator of the New Testament, that by His dying for the redemption of those transgressions which were in the former testament, they that are called might receive the promise of the eternal inheritance. For where a testament is, there must also be of necessity the death of the testator: For the testament is confirmed by the death of the party; otherwise it is of no strength so long as the testator is alive" (Heb. 9:15–17).

Thus we can be certain and assured by the death of Jesus Christ that His testament is available. So all our misdeeds can be pardoned, and we are made heirs of eternal life.

As a sign and pledge of this testament, He has left this divine sacrament instead of a certificate. It not only gives our soul the assurance of eternal salvation, but also it guarantees us the immortality of our body. Now it is enlivened by that immortal flesh of His. Thus in a certain way it comes to share in His immortality.

He who is partaker in this divine flesh by faith shall not perish (John 6:51). But to him that receives it without the same faith, it turns into a deadly poison. The apostle Paul says: "He, that eats of the bread and drinks of that cup unworthily, is guilty of the body and blood of the Lord," and "he eats and drinks his own damnation, because he does not discern the Lord's body" (1 Cor. 11:27, 29).

To say he "does not discern the Lord's body" is to presume that a

167

person partakes of the Lord's Supper without faith and charity. Since he does not believe that body is the Source of his life, nor the Cleanser of all his sins, he makes Jesus Christ to be a liar. He tramples underfoot the Son of God, not discerning the blood of the testament whereby he is sanctified. So he does a great wrong to the Spirit of grace and will be punished at God's hand for his unbelief and wicked hypocrisy. Since a hypocritic partaker does not trust in his justification by the passion of Christ, he really despises it. So he accuses himself, gives witness to his own iniquity, and condemns himself to eternal death by denying the life that God has promised him in that holy sacrament.

At times the Christian feels that his enemies want to overthrow him. This is when he begins to doubt whether he has received forgiveness of his sins by Jesus Christ. Then he is unable to withstand the Devil and his temptations, and the accusation of his own doubtful conscience also prevails against him. He begins to fear that hell will swallow him up, and that death will keep him in its eternal grip because of God's wrath.

When the real Christian feels these anxieties, let him return to celebrate the holy sacrament with a good heart and with a stout courage. Let him receive it devoutly. Let him say in his heart and answer his enemies thus: I confess I have deserved a thousand hells and eternal deaths because of the great sins I have committed. But when I reflect on this heavenly sacrament that I receive now, I am assured of the forgiveness of all my past misdoings and of my atonement with God for all time.

"If I look to my own deeds, there is no doubt that I must acknowledge myself to be a sinner and condemn myself. Nor will my conscience ever be quiet if I am tempted to think my sins are pardoned because of my good deeds. But when I look to the promises and covenant of God, He assures me of the forgiveness of my sins by the blood of Jesus Christ; I am certain I have been granted it and that I have His favor. I am certain of this, for He has made promises and covenants which cannot lie or deceive. Through this steadfast faith, I become righteous by Christ's righteousness" (Rom. 4:5, 24).

Has Christ not given His innocent body into the hands of sinners for my sins? Has He not shared His blood to wash away my iniquities? Why then are you so downcast, O my soul? Put your trust in the Lord. He bears you with such love that, to deliver you from eternal death, it pleased Him for His only Son to suffer death and passion. He has taken upon Himself to establish us in His strength. He has become mortal to make us immortal. He has come down to earth to raise us up to heaven. He has become the Son of Man with us in order to make us the children of God with Himself. "Who shall lay anything to the charge of God's elect? It is God that justifies. Who is he that condemns? It is Christ that died, yea rather, that is risen again who is even at the right hand of God, who also makes intercession for us" (Rom. 8:33–34).

The psalmist David also asked: "Why are you cast down, O my soul, and why are you disquieted within me?" (Ps. 42:5). Do you see nothing but the law, sin, wrath, heaviness, death, hell, and the Devil? Is there nothing to be seen of grace, remission of sins, righteousness, conciliation, joy, peace, life, heaven, Christ, and God? "Trouble me no more then, O my soul." For what is the law? What is sin? What is death and the Devil in comparison with these things? Therefore, trust in the God who has not spared His own dear Son. Instead God has given Him to the death of the cross for your sins and has given you the victory through Him.

This is the sweet doctrine of the Gospel that I desire all Christians to receive with thanksgiving and with an assured faith. For then Christ would be nothing but joy and sweetness to them. Then they would take heart in the victory of Christ's death, who was made a curse for us, subjected to wrath, weighed down by our person, and given our sins to carry upon His own shoulders. He made this blessed exchange by taking upon Himself our sinful person, and He has given us His perfection and victory so that we can now be clothed and free from the curse of the law.

Therefore every poor sinner can say with an assured confidence: "Christ, You are my sin and my curse; or rather I am Your sin and Your curse; and in contrast You have become my righteousness, my blessing and my life, my grace of God, and my heaven." If we by faith do behold this brazen serpent, seeing Christ hang upon the cross (John 3:14–15), then we shall see the law, sin, death, the Devil, and hell destroyed by His death. And so may we with the apostle Paul sing that joyful praise: "Thanks be to God who has given us the victory through our Lord Jesus Christ" (1 Cor. 15:57).

Thus it is with such faith and gratitude that we should receive the sacrament of the body and blood of our Lord Jesus Christ. In this way fear is driven out of the soul of the Christian. Charity is increased, faith is strengthened, the conscience is quieted, and the tongue will never cease to praise God and to give Him infinite thanks for so great a benefit. This is the virtue, advocacy, and only trust of our souls. This is the rock upon which the conscience is built; it fears neither storm, nor the Devil, nor any other thing.

Because the whole essence of the Eucharist depends upon the presence of the Christian at this divine sacrament, he must shut his eyes to all else and fix them upon the passion of our gracious Savior. On the one hand he beholds Him upon the cross laden with all our sins. Yet on the other side he sees God punishing, chastising, and whipping His only begotten and dearly beloved Son instead of us. Blessed is he who shuts his eyes to all other sights and will neither hear nor see any other thing than Jesus Christ crucified (1 Cor. 2:2). For in Him are laid up and bestowed all the treasures of God's wisdom and divine knowledge (Col. 2:3)! Blessed, then, is he who feeds his mind upon such divine food and who drinks of the love of God from such a sweet and unique chalice.

Before concluding this discussion, may I remind the Christian that Augustine was accustomed to call this holy sacrament the bond of charity and the mystery of unity. He said, "Whoever receives the mystery of unity, and regards not the bond of peace, receives not the sacrament for his own benefit, but rather as a witness against himself" (*Sermons on Time*, Part 11, Sermon 272).

Therefore we must understand that the Lord has ordained this holy sacrament not only to make us sure of the forgiveness of our sins, but also to stimulate us to have peace, unity, and brotherly charity. For in this sacrament the Lord makes us partakers of His body as He becomes one with us and we with Him. As He has but one body of which He makes us partakers, it is appropriate that we should also by such participation all become one body together among ourselves. Thus this union is represented by the bread of the sacrament. So, too, we must be joined together and united in such a harmony of mind that it will allow no division to creep in among us.

The apostle Paul shows us this unity when he says: "Is not the cup of blessing, which we bless, the communion of the blood of Jesus Christ? Is not the bread that we break the communion of the body of Jesus Christ? Whereas we being many, yet are we but one bread and one body, for as much as we be all partakers of one bread" (1 Cor. 10:16–17).

In this way, we understand that when we receive His most holy communion, we must consider that we are, all of us, grafted into Christ; we all become members of the self-same body, that is to say, of Jesus Christ. Therefore, we cannot offend, defame, and despise our own head, Jesus Christ.

Neither can we be at odds with any of our brethren; if so, we shall also be at odds with Him. Note how much care we take of our own body. So much then should we have for our own Christian brethren who are members of our body. Since no part of our body feels any pain without it spreading to all the other parts of the body, so should we hurt when our brother hurts and be moved also to compassion (1 Cor. 12:26).

It is with such thoughts that we should prepare ourselves for this holy sacrament and quicken our spirits with a fervent love toward our neighbor. For what greater incentive can we have to incite us to love one another than to see Jesus Christ. By giving Himself for us,

He not only prompts us to give ourselves for one another but also to make Him common to us all. Thereby He makes us all to be one in Him. So we ought to covet and seek to have in all of us but one mind, one heart, one tongue, and so be accorded and united together in thought, word, and deed.

We should also note that as often as we receive this holy and worthy sacrament, we pledge ourselves to all the duties of charity. We are not to offend any of our brethren or leave anything undone that may be profitable and helpful in their necessity. For if there are any who come to this heavenly table of the Lord that are divided and at variance with their brethren, they must recognize that they eat unworthily and are guilty of the body and blood of the Lord. They eat and drink their own damnation. For by their hatred and division from their brethren, they have once more rent asunder the body of Jesus Christ.

Let us go on, my brethren, to receive this heavenly bread and to celebrate the remembrance of our Lord's passion. May it strengthen and fortify the belief and assurance of forgiveness of our sins. May it quicken our minds and tongues to praise and exalt the infinite goodness of our God. Finally, may it cause us to cherish brotherly love and be a witness to the same unity that all of us have in the body of our Lord Jesus Christ.

PREDESTINATION

Besides prayer, the remembrance of baptism, and the frequent exercise of the most holy communion, the best remedy against diffidence and fear (which are not consistent with Christian love) is the reminder of our predestination and election to eternal life.

This truth is grounded upon the Word of God which is the sword of the Holy Spirit (Eph. 6:17). With it we may destroy our enemies. "Rejoice ye in this, says the Lord, that your names are written in heaven" (Luke 10:20). For there is no greater joy in this life, no greater comfort for the Christian who is afflicted, tempted, or fallen into any sin, than this: the remembrance of our predestination and the assurance that we are numbered among the names of those who are written in the Book of Life and who are chosen to be fashioned into the image of Christ.

How unspeakable is the comfort of this faith. How one can muse continually in one's heart upon this exceedingly sweet predestination. Hereby we may know that although we fall, God the Father, in His full knowledge, holds us up and reaches out His hands to us continually (Ps. 37:24)!

Such a soul can constantly say to himself, "If God has chosen me, and He predestinated me to the glory of His children, who can hinder me?" and "If God be with us," says the apostle Paul, "who can be against us?" (Rom. 8:31). Nay, in order that this predestination be accomplished in us, He has sent His dearly beloved Son; He is a most assured earnest and pledge to us that we have received the grace of the Gospel. For we are God's children, and we are chosen to have eternal life.

This holy predestination maintains the true Christian in a state of continual, spiritual joy. It increases his effort to do good works; it inflames him with the love of God; and it makes him an enemy of the world and of sin. Who could be fierce and hard-hearted when he comes to know that God in His mercy has made him to be His child from eternity? Will he not be more and more inflamed to love God?

Who could be so cowardly and lacking in courage to not esteem all the pleasures, all the honors, and all the riches of the world as filthy dung when he comes to realize that God has made him to be a citizen of heaven? Yes, these are they who worship God rightly "in Spirit and in truth" (John 4:23); they receive all things, whether prosperity or adversity, from the hands of God their Father. They will always praise and thank Him as their good Father for His righteousness and holiness in all His works.

Thus the Christian who is enamored with the love of God and armed with the assurance of his predestination will not fear death, sin, the Devil, or hell itself. Nor will such ever know what is the wrath of God. For such see nothing else in God but His love and fatherly kindness toward them. When they fall into any troubles, they will accept these as tokens of God's favor, and cry out with the apostle Paul: "Who shall separate us from the love of God? Shall tribulation, or distress, or persecution, or famine, or nakedness, or peril, or sword? As it is written, 'For Thy sake are we killed all the day long; we are accounted as sheep for the slaughter.' Nay, in all these things we are more than conquerors through Him that loved us" (Rom. 8:35–37).

Therefore it is not without reason that John says true Christians will clearly know they must be saved and glorified. Through this faith they become holy, just as Christ is holy (1 John 3:2–3). When the apostle Paul exhorts his disciples to a godly and holy life, he usually reminds them of their election and predestination (Eph. 1:4–6). For this is the most effective way to stimulate the love of God in true Christians and to promote good works. For the same reason, our blessed Lord Jesus Christ spoke openly of this most holy predestination (Luke 10:20). As One who knew how important this knowledge is, He spoke to edify His elect.

But perhaps you will argue with me and say, "I know quite well that those whose names are written in heaven have good reason to live in continual joy and to glorify God, both in word and in deed. But I do not know whether I belong to that number. So I live in perpetual fear. This is all the more so, because I know myself to be so exceedingly weak and frail as a sinner; I am unable to defend myself from the intensity of temptation which overcomes me every day. Moreover, as I see myself constantly afflicted and troubled with many temptations, I cannot help seeing the wrath of God afflicting me all the time."

My reply to you is to assure yourself that all these thoughts are only the temptation of the Devil. For he will seek every possible means to rob you of the faith and confidence that springs from faith; he tempts you to distrust the good will of God on your behalf. He endeavors to strip your soul of this precious garment. For he knows that no one is a true Christian unless he believes God's Word; it promises forgiveness of all sins and peace to all them that accept the grace of the Gospel.

So I say with assurance that whoever persuades himself that God is not a merciful and loving Father, nor is able confidently to accept the inheritance of the heavenly Kingdom from His hand with firm faith—this person is not faithful. Indeed, he makes himself completely unworthy of God's grace. In this regard the Apostle says that, "We are the temple of God, so far as we firmly maintain the confidence and glory of our hope until the end" (Heb. 3:6). In another place he exhorts us that we should not throw away our faith, "which has great recompense of reward" (Heb. 10:35).

Therefore, my beloved brethren, let us make every effort to do the will of God, like good children. Guard against sin as much as possible. Although we will sometimes fall into sin through our own frailty, let us not by such lapses assume that we are then vessels of wrath or that we are utterly forsaken by the Holy Ghost. For we have an Advocate, Jesus Christ, before God the Father, and He is the atonement for our sins (1 John 2:1).

Let us remember, brethren, the thought of Augustine who says, "None of the saints is righteous and without sin. Yet notwithstanding that, he does not cease to be righteous and holy so far as he retains His holiness with affection" (*Church Dogmatics*, 53). Therefore, if we are afflicted and tested, let us not think that God sends these trials because He is our enemy; rather it is because He is our loving Father. Solomon says: "The Lord chastens him whom He loves and scourges every child of His whom He receives" (Prov. 3:12).

Since we have received the grace of the Gospel and thereby have been received by God as His child, we must not doubt God's grace and good will toward us. And when we perceive ourselves delighting in God's Word and having a desire to follow the light of Jesus Christ, we must firmly believe that we are children of God and the temple of the Holy Ghost. For these things cannot be done by the power of man's wisdom. They are the gift of the Holy Spirit, who dwells in us by faith.

It is, as it were, a seal of authority which authenticates God's promises in our hearts. This certainty is impressed upon our minds. It is given to us by God as a pledge so that we are established and confirmed. "As soon as you believed [says the apostle Paul] you were sealed by the Holy Spirit of promise, who is the earnest of our inheritance" (Eph. 1:13–14).

In this verse he shows us that the hearts of the faithful are stamped with the Holy Spirit as if it were a seal. He calls the Holy Spirit "the Holy Ghost" or "the Spirit of Promise" since He confirms the promise of the Gospel. All we that believe in Christ, says the apostle Paul, are become the children of God (Gal. 3:26). "And because you are sons, He has sent the spirit of His Son into your hearts, crying, 'Abba, Father'" (Gal. 4:6).

Likewise to the Romans, Paul writes: "As many as are led by the Spirit of God, they are the sons of God. For you have not received again the spirit of bondage to fear, but you have received the Spirit of adoption, whereby we cry 'Abba, Father.' The Spirit itself bears witness to our spirit, that we are the children of God. And, if children, then heirs, heirs of God" (Rom. 8:14–17).

We should take note that in these two places, the apostle Paul speaks plainly by the Holy Spirit to assure those who receive the grace of the Gospel. If the Holy Spirit gives this assurance that we are God's children and heirs, why do we go on doubting about our predestination? The same writer says in the same epistle, "Whom He did predestinate, them He also called; and whom He called, them He also justified; and whom He justified, them He also glorified. What shall we then say to these things? If God be for us, who can be against us!" (Rom. 8:30–31).

Therefore, if I clearly recognize that God has called me, and has given me faith and its efficacy in my life (that is to say, peace of conscience, mortification of the flesh, and a quickening of spirit, either partially or wholly so), then why should I go on doubting whether I am predestined or not? So let us say with the apostle Paul that all true Christians "Receive not the spirit of this world, but the Spirit which is of God; that we might know the things that are freely given to us of God" (1 Cor. 2:12). How marvelous it is that we can know with certainty that God has granted us eternal life!

However, some will say no one should be so arrogant as to boast that he possesses the Spirit of God. They speak like this, as if the Christian is boasting of having election as his own reward and not simply because of the mercy of God. It appears to such a presumptuous act, to confess that one is a Christian. Yet behind this argument lies the assumption that one could be a Christian without having Christ's Spirit. So this argument overlooks the impossibility that we could never say that Jesus Christ is Lord (1 Cor. 12:3) or call God our Father unless the Holy Ghost moves our hearts and tongues to express such a wonderful reality. Yet those who consider us presumptuous in saying that "God has given us His Holy Spirit with faith" not only do not forbid us from saying every day "Our Father," but they even command us to do so!

But I have to ask them bluntly, "Is it possible to separate faith from the Holy Ghost since faith is the very work of the Holy Ghost?" If it is presumptuous to believe that the Spirit of Christ is in us (2 Cor. 13:5), why does the apostle Paul exhort the Corinthians to examine themselves to see whether they have faith? He affirmed them to be reprobates when they did not know if Jesus Christ was in them.

Indeed, it is great blindness to accuse Christians of presumptuousness when they celebrate the glory of the presence of the Holy Ghost. For without such glory in Christ there cannot be any Christianity at all. But Christ, who cannot lie, says that His Spirit is unknown to the world, and it is known only to those in whom He dwells (John 14:17). So let them learn to become good Christians, casting away their Jewish minds and embracing the grace of the holy Gospel. Then they will realize that real Christians have the Holy Spirit and know it in themselves.

But perhaps someone may argue that the Christian can never know he is in God's favor without some special revelation being given to him. Consequently, he can never know whether he is predestined or not. He may cite the words of Solomon: "No man knows either love or hatred by all that is before him" (Eccl. 9:1). He may also cite the words of the apostle Paul to the Corinthians: "I know nothing by myself; yet I am not hereby justified; but He that judges me is the Lord" (1 Cor. 4:4).

I think I have already explained quite clearly from other texts of Scripture that this opinion is false. So it only remains to show briefly that these two texts upon which this opinion is based should not be taken in this way.

With regard to Solomon's text, it is accurately translated. Yet anyone reading the context will not be so stupid that he does not understand him to say the following: If any man wants to judge whether God loves or judges him by the events of this life, he will labor in vain. For the same accidents which happen to the righteous also happen to the unrighteous; to him who makes sacrifices, as well as to him that sacrifices not. They happen to the good man as well as to the sinner. Therefore, it is clear that God does not always show His love toward those upon whom He bestows outward prosperity. On the contrary, He does not always show His displeasure toward those whom He will eventually punish.

So, my dear brother, does it seem reasonable to conclude that a man cannot be certain of God's grace simply because he cannot be certain of the vicissitudes of life that are temporary and transitory? A little earlier, Solomon has said that a man cannot discern any difference between the soul of man and the life of a beast, because both are seen to die the same way (Eccl. 3:19). Are we to conclude from this external accident that our belief in the immortality of the soul should be based merely upon conjecture? Surely not. But it is a waste of time to argue with such pretext against a truth that is so clearly known from the rest of Scripture.

As for the words of the apostle Paul, I see them in the context of what he was speaking about concerning the administration of the Gospel. He is not certain if he has made any mistakes; but in spite of this, he is not certain if he has really fulfilled all his duty to obtain the praise of righteousness before God as required of a faithful steward. Therefore he speaks of his office as a just and wise steward, not daring to justify himself or avowing that he has discharged his duty to the full and so satisfied his Lord's will. But he leaves it all to the judgment of his Lord. No one who reads these words of the apostle Paul and considers the context will doubt that this is their true meaning.

I know well that someone who expounds these words of the apostle Paul does not acknowledge he had any sin in himself; yet he did not know if he was righteous before God. As David affirms, no man can know his own sins perfectly (Ps. 19:12).

But these expositors do not notice that the apostle Paul bases righteousness not upon works, but upon faith (Rom. 3:28; 5:1, 18). For Paul utterly refuses to claim he has his own righteousness and embraces only the righteousness that God gives through Christ (Phil. 3:9).

Also, they do not consider that Paul was certain he was accepted for righteousness' sake by maintaining the soundness and purity of the Christian faith. He well knew that there was reserved for him a crown of righteousness (2 Tim. 4:8). He was also fully assured that no creature in heaven, earth, or hell was able to separate him from the love of God (Rom. 8:38–39). He longed to die, because he knew for a certainty that after his death he would be with Christ (Phil. 1:21–23).

All of these things would be false if Paul was not assured that he was righteous by faith and not by works. Therefore, my dearly beloved brethren, let us stop talking about the apostle Paul never having had this assurance. For he fought strongly against such assertions all the time. Throughout his ministry he emphasizes that righteousness is measured not by works but by faith in our Lord Jesus Christ.

Besides the two final authorities, Solomon and the apostle Paul, we could cite many other places in the Holy Scriptures which warn and encourage us to fear God; and yet they might seem contrary to the assurance of the predestination we have. If I would discuss them in detail, I should be too long-winded. But generally I can say that the fear of punishment was proper to the Old Testament, while the love of the child belongs to the New Testament. Accordingly, Paul testifies to this when he says to the Romans: "You have not received the spirit of bondage to fear, but you have received the Spirit of adoption, whereby we cry 'Abba, Father'" (Rom. 8:15). Likewise he says to Timothy that: "God has not given us the Spirit of fear, but rather of power and love" (2 Tim. 1:7). The Spirit of Jesus Christ has given us this promise by the mouth of the holy prophets, and brought it to pass, "That we, being delivered out of the hands of our enemies, may serve Him without fear before His holy presence, in all holiness and righteousness, all the days of our life" (Luke 1:70, 74–75).

In these and many other passages of Holy Scripture a man may clearly understand that painful and slavish anxieties are not consistent with the life of a Christian. This has already been confirmed when the Apostle declares that this spirit of fear is utterly contrary to spiritual cheerfulness and joy, the distinctives of the Christian. The apostle Paul shows this openly in writing to the Romans, saying: "The kingdom of God is righteousness, and peace, and joy, in the Holy Ghost" (Rom. 14:17). That is to say that every man who enters into the Kingdom of the grace of the Gospel has become righteous through faith. Afterwards he adds that there is peace of conscience which subsequently breeds such a spiritual, holy rest and gladness that the Apostle can encourage Christians to love joyfully (Eph. 5:19; Phil. 4:4). The apostle Peter also says that all they who believe in Jesus Christ do continually rejoice with an unspeakable and glorious joy, in spite of the diverse temptations with which they are afflicted (1 Peter 1:6, 8).

Therefore, when the Holy Scripture threatens and frightens Christians, they must understand that it speaks to such as are licentious. Since they are not thankful and honest as God's children, they must be handled as slaves. They must also be in awe until they come to taste and feel how sweet and pleasant the Lord is. Or they must be held in fear until such time as faith has had its effect upon them, and they begin to have the love that a child has.

So when the Scripture exhorts Christians to a true fear, it does not mean that they should fear the judgment and the wrath of God, as if it were already condemning them. The witness that the Holy Ghost gives to their spirit enables them to know that God has chosen them and called them of His own mercy, and not for their just deserts.

In this way the Spirit exhorts them away from a slavish fear toward the attitude which children have. Like good children they should be loath to offend against the Christian faith or to commit anything against the reality of being God's true children. Likewise they are sensitive not to grieve the Holy Ghost that dwells within them (Eph. 4:30).

Thus it is clear a man should truly see that a real Christian ought never to doubt his forgiveness of sins nor the reality of God's favor. Nevertheless, for the better satisfaction of the reader, I propose to outline the statements of some of the church fathers who confirm this truth.

Hilary of Poitiers says in his fifth canon upon Matthew: "It is God's will that we should hope without doubting His unknown will. For if the belief be doubtful, there can be no righteousness obtained by believing." And thus we see that according to Hilary, a man does not obtain forgiveness of his sins from God, except he undoubtedly believes that he will obtain it. "For he that doubts is like a wave of the sea, driven with the wind and tossed. Let not that one think that he shall receive anything of the Lord" (James 1:6–7).

Let us also listen to Augustine, who counsels us in his *Manual* to get rid of such foolish thought that would rob us of this devout and holy assurance. "Let such foolish thought," he says, "mutter as much as it wants. I know He is true to His promise and will keep His word; for He can do what He wills. And when I think upon the Lord's death, the multitude of my sins cannot dismay me, for I know in whom I have put all my trust. His death is my refuge; it is my salvation, my life, and my resurrection. It is the mercy of the Lord that is my desert. The more that He has the power to save, the more I am sure of being saved" (*Manual,* 23).

Elsewhere Augustine says that he would have utterly despaired because of his great sins and infinite negligences if the Word of God had not become flesh. Then he adds these words: "All my hope, all the assurance of my trust is placed on His precious blood which has been shed for us and for our salvation. In Him my poor life breathes. Confiding wholly in Him, I long to come unto You, O Father, not having my own righteousness, but that of Your Son, Jesus Christ" (*Manual,* 13). In these two places Augustine plainly shows that the Christian must not fear. But he can be assured of righteousness by grounding himself not upon his own works, but upon the precious blood of Jesus Christ. In this way he is cleansed from all sin and made to have peace with God.

Bernard of Clairvaux, in his first sermon upon the Annunciation (1, 1, 3), says quite explicitly that "it is not enough to believe theoretically that a man can have remission from his sins, apart from the action of God's mercy. Nor can any one good desire or human ability bring it about; not even one good work can do so. ... Nor would a man deserve eternal life by his own merits. Eternal life comes only if God gives a person the gift to so believe. In addition to all these things, which are only the beginning and foundation of our faith, it is necessary that you also believe that your sins are forgiven you for the love of Jesus Christ."

See then how this saintly Bernard confesses that it is not enough to believe generally in the forgiveness of sins. One must also believe particularly that his own sins have been forgiven him personally by Jesus Christ. The reason is ready at hand, namely that God has promised to accept you in righteousness through the merits of Jesus Christ. If, then, you do not believe that you have become righteous through Him, you only make God a liar. Consequently, you make yourself unworthy of His grace and mercy.

But you will say to me, "I truly believe in the forgiveness of sins, and I know that God is true. But I am afraid that I am not worthy to have such a great gift."

My answer is that the forgiveness of your sins will not be a gift of free grace but rather wages if God should give it to you because of the worthiness of your works. So I reply to you that God accepts you only for righteousness and does not lay your sin to your charge. The righteousness is only because of Christ's merits that are given to you and become yours by faith.

Therefore, following the saintly counsel of Bernard, believe that you not only have the forgiveness of sins in general, but believe also that you can apply the same belief to your own particular condition and person. You do so by believing without any doubt that all your own personal misdoings are pardoned through Jesus Christ. In doing so, you will give glory to God. By confessing Him to be merciful and true, you will become righteous and holy before God. For it is by the same confession that the holiness and righteousness of God shall be communicated to you.

Now we have come to the end of our discussion. The main purpose of writing this has been to praise and magnify the vast benefits of Christ crucified, which are offered to the Christian in spite of his limited abilities to understand it.

We have tried to demonstrate that faith justifies itself. That is to say, God receives as justified all those who truly believe that Jesus Christ has made atonement for their sins. However, as we have seen that light cannot be separated from the burning flame, no more can good works be separated from faith which alone justifies. It is this most precious doctrine that exalts Jesus Christ and humbles man's pride. Yet it is a doctrine that has and always will have opposition by pseudo-Christians who remain with "Jewish minds."

Blessed indeed is the reader, then, who imitates the apostle Paul by renouncing all his own self-righteousness and asking no other righteousness than that of Christ. Clothed in the garment of His righteousness, he can confidently appear before the presence of God (see Matt. 22:1–14). For then he will receive from God the blessing and the inheritance of heaven and earth, as well as His only begotten Son, Jesus Christ our Lord, to whom be all honor, praise, and glory, from this time forth forevermore. Amen.

CHRIST IS THE END OF THE LAW

A GUIDE TO DEVOTIONAL READING

"Wilt thou love God, as He thee! then digest,
My soul, this wholesome meditation,
How God the Spirit by angels waited on
In heaven, doth make His Temple in thy heart."
—*John Donne,* Holy Sonnet 15

If someone asked you if you were a "devotionalist" today, you would be excused for not knowing what he meant. If someone talked about being devotionally minded, you might raise an eyebrow in wonder.

This past century is possibly the first one in which action has been emphasized and valued more than contemplation. Today we do things. We think contemplation wastes time, produces nothing, and bumps awkwardly into our schedules. Devotional reading is a questionable priority for most successful people today.

But are we "successful" Christians if we are so busy organizing and propagating the Christian faith that we really do not know God personally—or intimately? Christian devotional reading helps us find intimate union with God. What is its motivation? To love God with all our heart, mind, and will.

DEVOTIONAL READING— A GREAT AWAKENING

The writer of Ecclesiastes realized that God set eternity within our hearts.[1] Augustine saw that God made man for Himself, and our hearts are restless till they find their rest in Him. This eternal yearning forms the basis of devotion.

We are created with infinite longings. We may try to conceal them and hide behind lesser values such as the recognition of beauty, or the desire for truth and authenticity. On the other hand, we may apologize for the adolescent ideals, incurable optimism, or indulgent romanticism connected with our longings. But once we have been awakened to heaven as a possibility, nothing else will do but to learn more about it. Then we are like pilgrims who have finally discovered where the Holy Grail is located. Or maybe we are like schoolboys. The mystery of mathematics is before us as we struggle to grasp the essentials of algebra and geometry, and we have to believe the teacher's enthusiasm that they do have intrinsic beauty.

We further discover that God's desires for us are not dissimilar from our truest, innermost desires for ourselves. Yet the connection between them at times seems terribly warped by selfishness and self-will. We reflect and we begin to see that the deepest form of nostalgia—to be loved, or to be understood, or to be reunited with the Infinite beyond all the universe—is "no neurotic fancy," according to C. S. Lewis. Rather it is "the truest index of our real situation."[2]

In Christ we also discover that it is not God's Personhood that is vague and intangible. It is our own personalities that are incoherent, bitty, and inadequate. So the reality of prayer in the name of Jesus is the search for a fuller, richer personality, the personality we most deeply long to have.

In this light we see devotional reading not just as a pious option to reading a good thriller or even a serious work. It is more in the nature of an awakening, as the Prodigal Son had at the swine trough. Our animal existence is simply not good enough when we discover inwardly that we have a royal Father and that we are made in the image and likeness of God.

The reading habits of the swine trough cannot ever satisfy a son and a swine at the same time. The reading habits of the "hired servants," guided by the mesmerization with "how-to" books which define life by action and buy acceptance by self-achievement, will not do either. For a beloved son or daughter, though a prodigal, responds to his or her acceptance in Christ. It is all we ever can "do." And it is more like lovers holding hands than corporate businessmen making decisions in the boardroom.

Indeed we find that life consists of a number of progressive awakenings. When we first study seriously, we are excited by the awakening of our mind's activity to reasoning and understanding in our world. We awaken again in the experience of taking responsibility for our lives when we have to be decisive about major acts or decisions. We awaken also when we are acted upon in suffering. For pain is a great awakener to realities that had previously slumbered in our lives. But it is the awakening to the love of God that transcends all other forms of human consciousness.

Today we are in grave danger of politicizing our faith, organizing it to death, and making it a cold ideology. We need once more to stand still and to see God. Then we shall begin to live again more like a child of God than like an entrepreneur before men. Deep emotions will be reopened. Memories will begin to be healed. The imagination will be redirected. And whole new possibilities will open out of dead-end streets to show us vistas of love and joy we never knew we could experience. Hope will succeed despair. Friendship will replace alienation. For we wake up one morning and discover we really are free to fall in love with God.

Then we can begin to understand what John Calvin meant when he called faith a firm knowledge of God's benevolence which is sealed in the heart. Calvin's affirmation recalled the burning heart in many a man before him: Jeremiah, the disciples on the Emmaus road, Augustine, Jonathan Edwards. This is how God instills the awareness that we are in the communion of saints, and that we are simply sharing what many others before us have already joyously experienced. We too, like them, now realize that heaven is our horizon after all.

DEVOTIONAL READING CHANGES HISTORY

Nothing can exceed the practice of prayer or the devotional reading of Scripture in one's daily devotions. Yet both of these practices need reinforcement and orientation from the example of others, from the sharing of their experiences. Perhaps the devotional use of Scripture is disappearing so fast that it can only be rediscovered and made common practice today with the help of other books. The results of such readings are often far-reaching. In fact, the accidental encounters with great classics of faith and devotion have triggered a whole series of unforeseen reactions.

This was so with C. S. Lewis. He came across such classics as the writings of Richard Hooker, George Herbert, Thomas Traherne, Jeremy Taylor, and John Bunyan as a result of his English studies.[3]

As a student, Alexander Whyte—the Scottish preacher of the late nineteenth century—undertook to index Thomas Goodwin's works of the seventeenth century. But he became so absorbed by them that, later in life, he wrote his *Spiritual Life* based on Goodwin's teachings. He confessed, "I carried his volumes about with me till they fell out of their original cloth binding, and till I got my bookbinder to put them into his best morocco. I have read no other author so much or so often."[4]

When John Bunyan married, his father-in-law gave him a dowry consisting of Arthur Dent's *The Plaine Man's Path-Way to Heaven* (1601) and Lewis Bayly's *The Practice of Pietie* (1613). Bunyan later acknowledged that these two works "beget within me some desires to Religion."[5] Their popularity clearly showed with many of his contemporaries.

One is also reminded of Ignatius of Loyola who, as a frivolous young knight, was wounded at the siege of Pamplona in 1521. There he was forced to spend his convalescence with only two books in his hands, *Life of Jesus Christ* by Ludolph the Carthusian and *Flower of the Saints* by Jacobine Varagine. These works left a deep impression upon him that led to a radical change of his life.

Christian friends deliberately introduced Augustine to the *Life of Antony*, which was written by Athanasius. This did not immediately impress Augustine, although his friend went on to tell him how at Trèves in Gaul a state official "read it, marveled at it, and was inflamed by it." While this official read, he began to think how he might embrace such a life of monasticism in the Egyptian desert. He thought about giving up his worldly employment to serve "You [God] alone …; and the world dropped away from his mind … while he was reading, and in his heart tossing thus on its own flood, at last he broke out in heavy weeping, saw the better way, and chose it for his own."[6]

Augustine adds a note about the result of reading such an example as Antony. This man and his companion were led to build "a spiritual tower at the only cost that is adequate, the cost of leaving all things and following You."[7]

The influence of mystical writers upon Martin Luther has been well documented. He read deeply the sermons of Johannes Tauler (1515–1516) and edited the anonymous mystical treatise which he entitled *German Theology* (1516, 1518). When he defended the ninety-five theses in 1518, he confessed that there was more good theology in Johannes Tauler's *Sermons*, more "pure and solid theology" than in all the works of scholasticism. Of *German Theology* he declared that "only the Bible and Augustine had taught him more about 'God, Christ, man, and all things.'"[8]

Sometimes the writings of mystics can prolong the struggles to know God personally. The readers are then caught up in their exercises and spiritual insights instead of in encountering God Himself. This was the case with John Wesley. From his mother he learned about many devotional works, especially when he first went up to Oxford as an undergraduate. He found the studies there, "an idle, useless interruption of useful studies, horribly and shockingly superficial."[9]

But Wesley was enchanted by Cardinal Fénelon's *Discourse on Simplicity;* it gave him the realization that simplicity is "that grace which forces the soul from all unnecessary reflections upon itself."[10] On vacation, his friend and spiritual guide Sally gave him a copy of Jeremy Taylor's *Rule and Exercise of Holy Living and Dying.* He admits that this volume "so sealed my daily practice of recording my actions (which I have continued faithfully until this moment) that I later prefaced that first *Diary* with Taylor's Rules and Resolutions. This helped me to develop a style of introspection that would keep me in constant touch with most of my feelings."[11] One wonders how far Fénelon and Jeremy Taylor contradicted the convictions of a confused young man.

About this time, Sally also encouraged John Wesley to read Thomas à Kempis's *Imitation of Christ.* This, too, made its mark upon him, and he determined to either belong to God or to perish. Yet these works in a sense only prolonged for some thirteen years the need for John Wesley to recognize that he must be "born again," and accept God as his own Savior. At the same time they left their mark indelibly upon his character and ministry.

Finally, we think of C. H. Spurgeon and of the profound influence that the Puritan writers had upon his whole life and preaching. He had a collection of some twelve thousand books, about seven thousand of them being Puritan writings. Over and over again, Spurgeon read *Apples of Gold* by Thomas Brooks. He also devoted much time to Brooks's *Precious Remedies Against Satan's Devices.* He delighted in all of Brooks's sweet devotional works.

But books by Thomas Goodwin, John Owen, Richard Charnock, William Gurnall, Richard Baxter, John Flavell, Thomas Watson, and of course John Bunyan, were also Spurgeon's companions.[12] Then in his own *Chat About Commentaries,* he confesses that Matthew Henry's *Commentary* on the Scriptures is his first selection as the Christian's constant companion. He recommended that all his students read it in the first twelve months after they had finished college.[13]

The influence of books upon Christian leaders and their impact in turn upon the renewal movements of the church is clear. As Richard Baxter pointed out in his *Christian Directory* in the seventeenth century, "many a one may have a good book, even any day or hour of the week, that cannot at all have a good preacher."[14]

Sometimes the book and the author are now totally unknown, yet their consequences have been conspicuous and permanent. Who reads today Arthur Dent's *Plaine Man's Path-Way to Heaven;* yet John Bunyan's *Pilgrim's Progress* has been translated into over 198 languages. Few know today of Florentinus of Deventer; yet his pupil, Thomas à Kempis, has had his book *Imitation of Christ* issued in over two thousand editions. Francisco de Osuna's *The Third Spiritual Alphabet* means nothing to most Christians now; yet it inspired Teresa of Avila's writings on prayer, writings that still influence us strongly. Nicholas Scupoli's *Spiritual Combat* (1589) was Francis de Sales's bedside reading along with the Bible for over sixteen years. Yet it is de Sales's own *Introduction to the Devout Life* that has had such profound impact on so many.

So the message is clear to us all. Open the windows of your soul in meditative reading, and the potentials of God's presence in your life can be, as Paul prays, "exceeding abundantly, above all that we can ask or think."[15]

THERE ARE NO INNOCENT READERS

There is no such thing as "just reading." Reading is an instrument also of our emotions and our spirit, our motives and our objectives. The monastic art of *lectio divina*, the practice of reading meditatively and prayerfully for spiritual nourishment and growth, is little known outside the Catholic traditions of spirituality today. The loss of such devotional assimilation of the Scriptures reflects upon the impatience many have with the spiritual readings of the great masters of Christian faith. Or it possibly shows the sheer neglect or ignorance of such works.

C. S. Lewis speaks of "the strange idea abroad that in every subject, the ancient books should be read only by the professionals, and that the amateur should content himself with the modern books ... a shyness," he adds, "nowhere more rampant than in theology."[16] But it would make a topsy-turvy confusion in Christianity if we were always contented with a shallow draught of what is said about its origins and never motivated to drink personally from the fountain source.

We are also guilty when we do not distinguish fundamental reading from accidental reading, or edifying reading from recreative reading. For they are all distinct.[17] Accidental reading is what catches our attention for the tactics of life so that we absorb a wide range of know-how, trivial and significant. All that is required of this kind of reading is mental mastery. Fundamental reading, that which we do strategically for training in a profession or discipline, demands docility and perseverance. The shift from the first to the second type of reading is from information to formation, and so the attitude of mind also changes.

Reading which relaxes is also tactical, yet it can catch us off guard sometimes. To absorb trivia which we label as "recreational" can be time wasted. Worse, it can take and divert our minds and spirits from the paths of righteousness and purity.

Such reading may really test our spirits and be evidence of the lack of a Christian imagination in our lives. Stimulating reading is dependent on more deliberate choices that we make. If we wish to be more sensual, then we will indulge in more of the pictorial pornography with which our society is so awash today. Or if we want to breathe the cleaner air of personal authenticity, we will enjoy good biography, be moved by the prayers or journals of great warriors of the faith, or even dwell in the parables of our Lord. It becomes an intense resource in times of depression to keep at hand favorite authors, inspiring pages, and familiar themes, to reinvigorate the flagging spirit.

We are not innocent readers, even when we choose not to read at all! We become guilty of blending our thoughts with the culture that we so readily accept. The TV set, for example, tempts us with deep, manipulative tendencies. For we can at the press of a button translate ourselves into a dozen different artificial environments. We can literally choose the environment we want to live in and live by. Are we not then also going to be tempted to manipulate our spiritual longings and needs also? Submission to the will of God seems to recede more than ever. This attitudinal revolution so deepens our egocentricity that listening to spiritual writers becomes hard indeed. Yet it is docility, not mastery, that is the essence of spiritual reading and the meditative life.

We also have a very short span of attention. Our style is disjointed: Our sentences break off readily, our messages are not always meaningful. We live to be entertained as a spectator rather than to be involved as a participant in life. Our books reflect the staccato of modernity. Messages are given in precise form and in shallow dosages. Likewise, our lifestyles change because procrustean man changes to each new fad and enthusiasm of the moment. It is a divorcing society, where one changes one's partner as one's mood also changes. The solid meat of the Word that the Apostle speaks of is rejected not just for milk but for cola. Classics of faith and devotion are not attractive to a generation that lives on a diet of popcorn and chewing gum.

We tend to live also on the externals of life. It is all showbiz and how we can impress other people. As Christians we are more concerned about the promotion of our faith than its private practice. Busyness is more significant than godliness. We are afraid to listen to God because we are more concerned about what other people think. The herd mentality and the tyranny of consensus—what Aldous Huxley once called "herd intoxication"—makes us afraid of solitude, of facing God alone, or indeed of our facing the inner feelings of guilt and self-betrayal.

Yet devotional reading is such a private, interior affair. It does require the moral courage of humility, of openness to life-changing perspectives, and of respect for my own inner being. It does mean shifting gears so that we operate with the fear of the Lord rather than be concerned about the fear of man.

We also play the numbers game. Everybody is doing it! we exclaim. How then can I, or should I, be odd man out?

In reply, Kierkegaard would ask us to deliberate: "Do you now live so that you are conscious of yourself as an individual?"[18] Above all, do you realize the most intimate of relationships, "namely that in which you, as an individual, are related to yourself before God?"

In nature there does seem to be a prolific waste of sunlight, of plants, of lesser and greater animals in the great food chains of our ecosystems. In the callousness of man's violence against his fellows, numbers still do not seem to matter. In our disobedience to the voice of conscience, our personal reading habits, prayer life, and lack of spiritual progress also do not seem to matter if we see Christianity as the crowd.

But God does not judge as the crowd. Rather, as a Father He knows the fall of every sparrow; every hair of our head is counted by Him. "In eternity you will look in vain for the crowd ... in eternity you, too, will be forsaken by the crowd."[19] This is terrifying unless we prepare for eternity by meeting with God now, constantly and longingly.

Devotional reading helps us, then, to have an eternal consciousness, not a herd consciousness; it is the primary consciousness of man before his Maker, and of me before my Savior. "In eternity," adds Kierkegaard, "there are chambers enough so that each may be placed alone in one ...

a lonely prison, or the blessed chamber of salvation."[20] Is then my spiritual reading and its reflection helping me to see myself "in place," in the will and love of God? True individualism is not following the fashion, but following God.

THE PLACE OF INTIMACY WITH GOD

It is no coincidence that the theme of "following God" for the Israelites in the Exodus was a desert experience. Our desert is not normally the Sahara or the Gobi, or even the great Australian Outback. Our desert is the space to reflect on our shattered dreams, the alienation no touch can connect between even loved ones, the trackless uncertainty of tomorrow, and the experience of inner darkness. There God calls us to Himself, not from our usefulness but for ourselves.

When we say yes to God, He then takes us into the desert. There are no clear directions, nothing systematic, no concrete proposals, no exciting blueprints, no promising opportunities; there is just the promise to be unafraid to be. It is surrender, utterly so. It is docility, whatever the cost. It is divine companionship, regardless of the consequences.

Carlos Carretto acknowledged that the great gift the desert gives us is prayer.[21] The desert is the place of silence before God where the quietness makes the heart's awareness of His presence come closer than our own breathing. In this silence of attentiveness, we listen to God speaking through His Word. Silence becomes stale without the Word, but the Word loses its recreative power without the silence of the desert.

The desert experience is not just an environment for stoicism. It is the place of intimacy with God. It needs the quiet withdrawal—at least temporarily—from the world of men to be alone with God. It is a reflective dwelling place where one sees things in the light of eternity and therefore in true proportions. It is the removal from agitation, bustle, and speed to see things in stillness. It is where we silence our passions and recede from our tensions. Like a desert wanderer, we learn to discover the oasis where searching is no longer necessary. There we rest, refreshed and renewed.

The desert life has a way of reducing needs to the bare essentials of water, food, and shelter. In the desert alone with God we discover He is enough to satisfy every need. Our only remaining need is simply to need Him more. Of all the lessons the desert teaches, none is greater than finding the intimacy of God.

No wonder, then, that some of the most vital literature of spiritual renewal has come from the Desert Fathers—Antony, Athanasius, Origen, Pachomias, Evagrius, Basil, Gregory of Nyssa, and many unknown men whose sayings we still treasure. What later became institutionalized as "monasticism" is none other than the reflection on the desert life alone with God. We are reminded that without the desert experience of self-emptying, of detachment from idolatry, of surrender in commitment to God, and of our spiritual awakening to God, devotional reading has no significant part to play in our lives. For these are the basic motives and desires needed for devotional reading.

Space and time are required to actualize the desires for the desert. "The quiet time" is either a pious blank in the morning, or it is the most important space in our daily lives. Our bedtime reading is another time for our devotions. Fixed moments during the day give devotion spiritual reality.

Emotionally, too, our desert experiences are not just the spaces God should be invited to fill; they are reminders of what He really wants to occupy in our lives. Indeed, our solitude is the space in which we are conscious of needing Him. Devotional literature will help us to see what an expanding universe His presence should fill. This is the measure to which we see spiritual progress—our increasing neediness for God. This is not weakness but the secret of our greatest strength.

However, a journey into the desert requires a guide, in case we get lost. We need guidance lest we succumb to its dryness of discouragement and defeat. In the same way, our spiritual journey requires a guide.

Supremely we have the Holy Spirit as our Guide. But His presence depends also upon the condition that we do not grieve Him nor quench Him. We therefore have the counsels, inspiring examples, and the spiritual experiences of God's people to help guide us. For church history is properly the actualization of the communion of saints whose faith we are exhorted to follow.

The shallowness of much contemporary Christian life is its modernity. We need all twenty centuries of the life of devotion to help us become devotees of Christ at the beginning of the twenty-first century.

So let us learn to enjoy the communion of saints, reliving their lives, rethinking their thoughts, and reexpressing the ardor and fervor of their desires for God. When we get discouraged, these examples of the past show us that when Christian ideals are really tried, they will bear rich fruit. Their devotional writings can revitalize the lifelessness of our formalities like the dry bones in desert wastes that became revitalized in Ezekiel's vision. In another metaphor, Paul speaks of the cloud of witnesses that cheer on the athlete in the race. Devotional works do just that; they encourage us on to the finishing post.

READING GUIDELINES WHICH ARE LIFE-CHANGING

In spite of the spate of new books and of reprints of spiritual literature, there is little guidance offered as to how the art of spiritual reading can and should be cultivated. We have hinted already that the art of devotional reading is not exegetical, not informational, and not literary in its emphasis. Spiritual reading is essentially formative of the soul before God. We need, then, to read it in such a way that it helps us to be inspired and in tune with God in the "inner man." For it is writing that turns us heavenward, and it is formative of our character in Christ.

1. Spiritual reading requires a primary emphasis on the devotional use of Scripture.

Do not allow the first excitement of tasting devotional literature to detract you from the priority that you should still give to Bible study and meditation. Remember, the Scriptures are the canon of the devotion of God's people. They saw the Scriptures uniquely as the final revelation of God's purposes for man. They saw the Scriptures guided by the Holy Spirit.

However, what needs recovery or significant revision in the spiritual exercises of many Christians is how to use and meditate upon the Bible devotionally. For we have tended since the Reformation to flatten the interpretation of Scripture into the one process of historical criticism; we want to see it as we believe the text to have been originally written by the author. The medieval scholar-monk saw it, however, much more richly, as the following hermeneutical rhyme summarizes its fourfold meaning:

"The letter shows us what God and our fathers did;
The allegory shows us where faith is hid;
The moral meaning gives us rules of daily life;
The analogy shows us where we end our strife."

While we do not systematically look for such fourfold levels in every verse of Scripture, nevertheless the literal or plain meaning of the text, as we believe it to be, requires also the use of symbolism to remind us of its mysteries. The use of moral application for the individual believer is also required, as well as the awareness of the transcendent realities of eschatology hidden in the text. This treatment is best seen in the Psalter, which has always been the most popular book of the Bible in the liturgical readings of the Church.

2. The art of devotional reading is less a matter of techniques than it is a matter of attitudes of the heart.

Taking note of the pressures and obstacles of our culture that would negate and sterilize the values of devotional reading is like developing a "sixth sense." It is a process akin to developing spiritual discernment and desire. It is clearly different from the curiosity for more information or the intellectual challenge to master rational understanding. The attitude is changed from a longing for information to a willingness to be reformed and a desire to be transformed. The creation mandate to have dominion over the earth by the *imago dei* is surpassed when we move to the redemptive mandate to be conformed to the image of Christ.

This involves a new way of knowing with a different mind-set. Informational reading is more a search for questions and answers. Devotional reading dwells more on the basic issues of living before God. The former looks for transparency in understanding, the latter is living contentedly with mysteries in appreciation and adoration. Again, informational reading is more dialectical and comparative; logic is important. But devotional reading is more docile and receptive rather than critical and comparative.

Informational reading tends toward being dissective. Data are taken to pieces by analysis in order to increase the range of one's ability to learn new things in new arrangements. But devotional reading is the readiness to leave all initiative in God's hands, to recollect and wonder at what God has already done, and to be united with God in living and dynamic ways. It is like the captain of the ship inviting the pilot to take the bridge. For this reason, devotional reading is much more personal and involves self-surrender, docility, and a willingness to change course in deep resolutions and by inner disciplines. The keeping of a spiritual journal may now begin to mark the changes of attitudes and of the desires before God.

Such devotional reading which encourages changes of character may therefore encounter severe spiritual battles and deep emotional struggles. It will require gentleness of spirit to avoid guilt-trips, to sustain enjoyment of spirit, and to avoid being unrealistically harsh with one's self. It will require patience and the long view of Christ's control of our lives.

3. Devotional reading has more of the character of a spiritual awakening out of cultural sleep than it has the idea of improving existing attitudes.

We readily "sleep" within our culture until we travel abroad and are surprised by how differently other societies live and behave. The Apostle implies we need to spiritually awaken out of our cultural conformities, mind-set, and attitudes that we share with the world around us; we need to live to God freshly and honestly (1 Thess. 5:6). Often this requires a renewed brokenness of spirit, a new or deepened sense of sin, or a profound reevaluation of our priorities. Then we begin to discover two Christians can share the same orthodoxy of doctrine and yet have profoundly differing attitudes of spirit.

Much distress and confusion in the church today demands all the more discernment of attitudes among Christians to avoid what Bonhoeffer called "cheap grace" and to exercise true devotion before God. We may need then to "travel abroad" as the Desert Fathers did when they left the cities of men. We may need to explore as the medieval mystics explored, or suffer as the Puritans suffered, in order to learn how secular their contemporary species of Christianity really was, and ours is today.

Confession and repentance must therefore be the consequences of devotional reading. It stirs the heart too uncomfortably to be ever confused with entertaining reading. It is too radical to leave us safe within the sphere of our own mastery and control of new information. For the pathology of the heart is revealed in its deceptions, its hiddenness of sin, and in sin's inability to be controlled.[22]

Confession, then, implies both the need to acknowledge (*confiteri*) the holiness of God and to make confession (*confessio*) of guilt and sin.[23] Only sacrifice can unite the sinner with God, and the only sacrifice that unites man with God is that of Jesus Christ. The value of all other sacrifices derives from this. Then confession becomes praise, a thanksoffering. So Bernard of Clairvaux exhorts us, "By the confession of sins and by the confession of praise, let your whole life confess Him!"[24] With praise as a garment, confession becomes the act of one who has recovered an inner beauty, the budding of glory to come.

If we think of some spiritual writers such as Thomas à Kempis in his *Imitation of Christ* as too astringent and severe, could it be that our own lives are not confessional enough? Could it be that they are therefore lacking adequate praise? For praise flows out of gratitude, and gratitude springs out of confession of sin in the realization of who God is. Contemporary theological expression of faith as a belief system has come a long way from twelfth-century men such as John of Fecamp, who regarded theology as primarily a task of praise, adoration, and prayer, touched off by the contemplation of God.[25]

It is in the confession of sin that we discover new dimensions of self and of self-love that need to be dealt with. An awakening to the consciousness of indwelling sin in the believer such as that so vividly exposed by John Owen gives a new sensitivity to the reality of Satan that drives us to our knees. Temptation becomes a deeper reality that requires more moral wakefulness in more devotional reading.[26] Repentance becomes a lived reality that needs the support and comfort of the communion of saints.

So a desire to reset our course of life after failure and dishonesty with our own soul will intensify our search to learn from others how they dealt with these issues. Seeing life now with deeper meaning calls forth greater spiritual resources than we previously ever imagined we would need. Once in pilgrimage and away from the status quo, we are on a long journey. We have awakened out of a long, dull sleep. Like John Bunyan's Christian, we shall need many spiritual companions.

4. Devotional reading has its own pace, a slower pace.

Once we have begun to see discipleship as a long obedience, then we have to resist the impatience of our "instant society." If our devotional reading is to be life-changing and life-forming, we cannot look for instant results. It is, therefore, futile to rush through a devotional work in a hurry. Unlike an Agatha Christie novel, we cannot get through it in an evening.

Much inauthenticity arises in our lives because we do not differentiate speeds; we do things too fast. As it is, I think faster than I can talk, I talk faster than I can act, and I act faster than I have character for so many actions. So I tend always toward the inauthentic.

Spiritually, we need to slow down and spend more time in reflection and silence. We need the slowly measured pace of regular, fixed times of reading, even if this is only fifteen or thirty minutes a day. To absorb a few lines of a writer in one's heart and through the bloodstream of one's attitudes is far more effective than to anxiously speed-read merely for the sake of curiosity. If the problem of many churches is how the speed of boardroom decisions can be communicated in a community spirit, then the problem of devotional reading is how the impatience of the mind can be restrained from its lust for more information.

Space, as well as time, is required for devotional reading. Literally this may lead to the habit of developing a particular environment, an area in one's room that locates an "altar" of devotion. Physically it may require a comfortable posture, perhaps a particular chair, where one can most readily relax and where an atmosphere is created specifically for such exercises of devotion as prayer and contemplation. It may be that we should first take spiritual reading seriously when we are on holiday or vacation; there we sense the relaxing, recreational atmosphere of spaciousness we need for such spiritual exercises and disciplines. A facetious advertisement reads on a Los Angeles freeway, "With ice cream every day can be a sundae." The truth is that, with every day nurtured by spiritual reading, all days are Sundays.

5. Choose classics of faith and devotion from a broad spectrum of God's people.
We have noted that the poverty of Christendom today requires the resources of all twenty centuries of spiritual traditions, be they Orthodox, Catholic, or Protestant. Need we hesitate, then, to receive the diverse and catholic range of experiences that other saints of God have experienced throughout the ages and across the cultures of mankind? Indeed, those who experience most of the riches of God's grace can most afford to be eclectic in their spiritual reading. This they can do without losing in any way their firmness of faith and doctrine, nor be in any way careless with the essential truth of the Gospel.

An example of how such wide reading can enrich a Christian is exemplified in the life and ministry of Dr. Alexander Whyte, an influential member of the Free Church of Scotland, a church not known for its catholic interests. When he was fifty-six years old (1892), Alexander Whyte began to read the collected works of William Law. He wrote an anthology of Law's works in his book *The Characters and Characteristics of William Law*. In the preface he said of this Anglican, "The study of this quite incomparable writer has been nothing else than an epoch in my life."[27]

Then Whyte was led to study Teresa of Avila of whom he also wrote. He wrote other tributes of Lancelot Andrewes, Sir Thomas Browne, Samuel Rutherford, and the Russian Father John of Cronstadt. In a period of seven years, Alexander Whyte came to see a vast new vista of spirituality in writers whom he had never known before. So he began to realize that the admiration and love of the great saints of God is indeed a study of great worth.

"Exercise the charity," Whyte used to exhort, "that rejoices in the truth," wherever it is found, and however unfamiliar may be its garb. "The true Catholic, as his name implies, is the well-read, the open-minded, the hospitable-hearted, the spiritually-exercised Evangelical; for he belongs to all sects, and all sects belong to him."[28]

6. Enjoy spiritual friendships with soul-friends so that you can mutually benefit in a group study or in a shared reading program.

Such a group can meet every two or four weeks to hear and discuss books reviewed in turn by members of the group. At first, such reading may intensify deep spiritual challenges and generate a whole new sense of awareness to realities. It is a common reaction to question one's self whether one is becoming unbalanced or even crazy to have such convictions and longings. For just as the recovery from a severe illness, the threat of death, or an experience of deep brokenness may open up new doors of perception, so the fresh challenge of reading Christian mystics may do the same. It is then very important to be encouraged and led on wisely by those more experienced. Moreover, differing reactions give one a sense of proportion or correct one-sided impressions. The common goal of growing up into Christ, argues the apostle Paul, is a corporate maturity (see Eph. 4:13–14).

A spiritual friend, says the twelfth-century writer Aelred of Rievaulx in *Spiritual Friendship,* is one who is loyal and has right motives, discretion, and patience in order to help his friend know God better.[29] Since there is no end to the extent to which I can and do deceive myself, I need a spiritual guide to keep me honest. Moreover, the love of God is only effectively developed when my friend helps to draw me out of myself and to show me how I can enter into a wider circle of insights where I can be more honest with myself.

Thus revelation and honesty can give shape to spiritual companionship. Spiritual life rests upon revelation: the revelation of Christ who continually calls us in the power of the Holy Spirit into a relationship with Him. It rests on honesty: honesty with regard to what is there to be seen and to be reckoned with. So spiritual companionship is a process of both nurture and of confrontation, both of which are helped by reading and the discovery of devotional literature together.

A true friend in Christ will wake me up, help me to grow, and deepen my awareness of God. For God's love is mediated through human relationships, by those who care for me, encourage me, and desire my affections to become God-centered. Indeed, says Aelred, God is friendship, and so friendship with the spiritually-minded will lead me toward godliness. Perhaps few of us today take spiritual friendship quite so seriously.

7. Recognize that spiritual reading meets with obstacles that discourage, distract, or dissuade you from persistence in your reading.

Often we are not discerning enough to see or to question why a book may not grip our immediate attention, or why it seems so irrelevant to us. It may be caused by our own despondency or spiritual state as referred to earlier. Discouragement may rear its ugly head even when there are clear signs that we are being blessed. What the Desert Fathers called "accidie," boredom, flatness, or depression, may also be our affliction when we are tempted to believe we are making no spiritual progress at all.

We may also be distracted from reading the Fathers because we have never learned to live by a book; the book has meant only entertainment. After a casual flicking through TV programs, concentrated reading is perhaps a new discipline. Or perhaps we have never known the experience of awe and wonder in the presence of God, such as some spiritual reading will incite. This attitude may therefore need development before we enjoy some of the spiritual masters.

We may also be dissuaded from going far into the spiritual classics because of their time-bound cultural and theological frame. For instance, the fourfold levels of exegesis of medieval use of Scripture needs some understanding and sympathy before the sermons of

Bernard of Clairvaux may mean very much to us today. Middle English mystics such as the unknown author of *The Cloud of Unknowing*, Richard Rolle, Margery Kempe, Walter of Hilton, or others make it difficult for us when they insist we put away all human thought in our contemplation of God. They argue it is love rather than reason itself which gives such true understanding. They speak of "discretion," a spiritual sensing of grace, humility, contrition, and deep contemplation of God that is truly required.

Even later literature such as that of the Puritans may put us off because of their Latinized style or their "precision" in tabulating major and minor headings.[30] One can understand their nickname of the "Precisians" in the ways they often categorized point after point. It is for this reason of changed vocabulary, loquaciousness, changes in style, etc., that we have undertaken to rewrite in more contemporary fashion some of these classics, a task many other publishers and editors are also now undertaking. So there is little excuse today for the modern reader to say such material is unintelligible or unascertainable.

It is, of course, true that the literary imagery of such works is often that of a bygone culture. Bernard's *In Praise of New Knighthood*, or Teresa of Avila's *Interior Castle*, or Bunyan's *Holy War* may seem like out-of-date symbols. Yet they also contain principles for spiritual warfare, for the surrender of self to the communion with God, or for watchfulness in temptation; they remain as timeless principles. For mortification always remains a vital exercise, or series of exercises, in the Christian's life.

8. Seek a balance in your reading between modern and ancient writings.
Remember that modern writing is untried, lacks vintage, and often reflects the fads of the marketplace. As C. S. Lewis has said:

A new book is still on trial, and the amateur is not in a position to judge it. ... The only safety is to have a standard of plain, central Christianity ("mere Christianity" as Baxter called it), which puts the controversies of the moment in their proper perspective. Such a standard can only be acquired from old books. It is a good rule, after reading a new book, never to allow yourself another new one till you have read an old one in between. If that is too much for you, you should read an old one to every three new ones.[31]

In spite of such a precaution, when *Christianity Today* did a popular survey of "100 Select Devotional Books" (September 25, 1961), less than one-third were over a hundred years old. Most that were chosen were contemporary works. Rightly excluded were works of general religiosity such as the popular books of K. Gibran, works of speculative mysticism such as those of Meister Eckhart or Jakob Boehme, works reflecting contemporary positive thinking, or works of sweetness and light, all of which types have an unrealistic view of sin in human life.

At the same time, many of us may find the need for some entry point into a deeper spiritual experience by the use of modern writers who clear the trail to follow beyond the secular, modern mind and back to the ageless truths of Christianity. C. S. Lewis himself needed the sanity and humor of G. K. Chesterton, as well as the Christian imagination of George MacDonald, to feed him symbolically. Then he could go back to Boethius's *The Consolation of Philosophy* which gave Lewis a firm awareness of the solidity of eternity that was more than measureless time. But it is typical of life-shaping literature that very few authors really can do this for us. So Lewis would assure us, as so many have experienced this, that reading too widely may leave very little profound effect, however broadly we may become informed.

For many today, Michel Quoist's book *Prayers of Life* has revolutionized their prayer life and brought life and humanity into their devotions. I was stirred first of all in the challenge of Soren Kierkegaard's *Purity of Heart Is to Will One Thing*. It shakes one to the roots to mean business with the Almighty. P. T. Forsythe in *The Soul in Prayer* reminds us that "the worst sin is prayerlessness." Oswald Chambers in *My Utmost for His Highest* has lifted many on to the spiritual quest. At the same time, no devotional book, past or present, can do anything decisive if we are not already longing for a deeper spiritual life and prepared to receive it.

Just as there are psalms for all the moods and needs of life, so there should be a balance in our reading. Sometimes we may need the solid theological reading of Calvin's *Institutes*. At other times the joyous celebration of Thomas Traherne's *Centuries*, or the poems of George Herbert's *Temple*, are more suitable. John of the Cross combines some of the finest lyrics in Spanish literature with expressions of the most intense suffering and fervor for God in *Dark Night of the Soul*. The hymns of John and Charles Wesley, or the *Journal* of George Whitefield, or the *Letters* of Fénelon, or the *Pensées* of Pascal, cover rightly varied expressions of the soul before God. The diversity aids balance in our spiritual diet.

9. Accompany your spiritual reading with the keeping of a journal or some reflective notebook.

The Puritans used to argue that as the captain of a ship kept his log, or as the doctor recorded his case studies, or as a businessman audited his accounts, so the Christian should keep accounts with God; indeed daily, short accounts.

Indeed, from this tradition of keeping a journal we have some of the great treasures of spiritual literature. We think of John Bunyan's *Grace Abounding to the Chief of Sinners*, the *Memoirs* of David Brainerd, the Quaker journals of men such as George Fox and John Woolman, the journals of John Wesley and George Whitefield. Their examples still encourage us not just to record spiritual successes, but note also the goodness of God in our failures, depressions, and recoveries. They also point us to the consideration of small matters that may seem trivial and unimportant, yet are also maintained within the provident care of God. Likewise, there will be times when our aridity of spirit may appear to make our devotional study and meditation pointless and useless. Then it is that the faithful and sustained recording is kept up as a labor of love, and we honor Him in all circumstances.

Writing things down is also a helpful, reflective exercise. It often helps to clarify thoughts when our emotions are confused or lazy; it

helps to keep things memorable and edifying. The fruits of our meditations are also preserved when "wonderful thoughts" could so easily
evaporate again.

For some, keeping a journal seems too grand an exercise for their diary
jottings. Others may never get into the habit of having one either.
Nevertheless, their spiritual autobiography is still vital to them, for they
have been taught to see every significant event as happening since their
conversion. In some circles this can lead to an unhealthy emphasis on a
once-for-all experience that settles past, present, and future in such a way
that no spiritual progress is ever made subsequently. It all happened once
and for all. No, if we are pilgrims, then life still lies open before us, and so
our spiritual autobiography is still in the making. Premature attempts to
finish the "story" either at conversion, at a "second blessing," or at the
reception of a specific gift or insight should be resisted.

Perhaps, then, we need to exercise more sense of a spiritual autobiography in our lives, either by journal keeping, diary jottings, memoirs, or
just an ongoing list of gratitude for the many events God has transformed in our experiences. But we do need to be guarded by too frequent
expression of public testimonies which can be exaggerated or spiritually
wasted by overexposure. Dostoevsky's hero in *Notes from Underground*
argues that "consciousness is a disease."[32] The self-fulfillment cult of this
"me-generation" certainly is a deadly plague among us today. Perhaps
the recovery of spiritual autobiography will help us. For all autobiography is a search for a meaningful pattern to life, and all such quests are
doomed to futility without reference to our Creator and Redeemer. For
the absence of God from our thoughts and decisions, desires and
delights, is that which makes self-consciousness so often demonic.

The keeping of a journal around our devotional reading will thus help
to maintain our reading as a steady diet. It may also be a form of self-
direction in the cultivation of conscience, a knowledge with God rather
than knowledge on my own. It is a way of living that prepares us for
heaven. Bishop Joseph Hall, who recorded many of his meditations,
reminds us that such reflections so recorded are "the Christian's heavenly
business, for it is no more possible to live without a heart than it is to be

devout without meditation."[33] Such meditative recording will remind us constantly of the long journey of the soul before God.

10. Choose carefully the devotional work that you desire to read for life-changing benefits to your soul. Pray seriously and seek someone to help you in the quest.
There is such a range of books available of a spiritual character that you may be discouraged at the beginning by the very variety. So first of all, distinguish between the "primary" classics that are basic reading from the supportive "secondary" sources that are only minor classics. We may then call "tertiary reading" the background histories of spirituality, biographies, and other material that help to fill out the context of the primary classics. The "fourth" kind of reading is the vast range of contemporary devotional literature which has not yet been sorted out as having permanent or passing interest and value.

Do not imitate someone else's choice of a classic, because your needs may be very distinct. So the advice of a spiritual friend may be needed to help you discover the right book that may remain as your friend for life. If you are still without such a spiritual guide, the following suggestions may help.

If you feel that your worst enemies are still inside you—guilt, lust, a constantly defeated Christian life—then Augustine's *Confessions* may just be the book for you. Many of us will identify with Augustine's recognition that he really postponed exploring and submitting to Christianity because he really wanted his lust for sex, beauty, and success to be satisfied rather than cured. "Lord, make me chaste, but not yet." Augustine's honesty and openness before God are so refreshing and relieving to a lifetime of bottling things up and postponing that catharsis of soul which many of us need so badly.

If you mean business with God, and have felt the absence of a real discipleship before God, then Thomas à Kempis's *Imitation of Christ* may be the astringent call you are looking for. The tradition out of which this small work arose was the notes (*ripiaria*) or collection of sentences from the Scriptures and the Fathers that became a focus for meditation, not only for

Thomas à Kempis but for countless generations of "the committed ones." Why not join the august band of devotees?

If you see life as a constant struggle, and feel tempted to give up in discouragement and weakness, then perhaps Lorenzo Scupoli's *Spiritual Combat* is your need. Second only to *Imitation of Christ*, it has had the most profound influence, especially in eastern Europe, since it was published in 1589. Francis de Sales kept it by his bedside for sixteen years, "the golden, dear book" that he read every day. For those needing to be gentle with themselves in self-rejection, Francis de Sales's own meditations, *Introduction to the Devout Life,* is a sweet bouquet of daily refreshment for many sensitive spirits.

Falling in love with God seems a fearful thing for many Christians. Perhaps one begins this experience by reading the classic of Jean Pierre de Caussade, *Abandonment to Divine Providence.* It was recently retranslated by Kitty Muggeridge as *The Sacrament of Every Moment* and has the same theme as this work. Brother Lawrence's *The Practice of the Presence of God* is in the same tradition of seventeenth-century French devotion.

All this may encourage you to return to the twelfth century, which like our own today was much preoccupied with the discovery of the individual through romantic love. The response of Bernard of Clairvaux and his friends was to see the love of God as the source of true personhood. Man's being calls out for love, and love's source is God Himself. Our integrity and deepest understanding of ourselves deepen when we fall in love with God as a permanent reality. So short works such as *On Loving God, Spiritual Friendship,* and meditations on the *Song of Songs* helps us to enter into this reality.[34]

If you feel the need to nurture your devotional life with solid theological study also, then it is often overlooked that Calvin's *Institutes,* part three, is written precisely for that purpose. Before you get there, you may find it helpful to read William Wilberforce's *Real Christianity,* a spirited attack on civil religion by the abolitionist leader against slavery.[35] If your theology may be clear, but your feelings are still confused and weak toward God, then Jonathan Edwards's *Treatise on the Religious Affections* remains unique in this need of disciplined desires for God.[36]

This is a book that requires much recovery for post-modern man.

Perhaps we also need to return to books of childhood, such as Bunyan's *Pilgrim's Progress*, to see at deeper levels what is timeless for all generations. Recovering our childhood for God may help us redeem the past for future enrichment as C. S. Lewis did with the tales of George MacDonald. Prejudices of childhood sometimes need to be unfrozen by rereading sources that previously blocked our progress.

In his *Maxims*, John of the Cross sums up what we have attempted to say. "Seek by reading, and you will find meditating; cry in prayer, and the door will be opened in contemplation."[37] But he admits, they who are "pilgrims for recreation rather than for devotion are many." So he warns us, "Never admit into your soul that which is not substantially spiritual, for if you do so, you will lose the sweetness of devotion and recollection." He adds, "Live in the world as if God and your soul only were in it; that your heart may be captive to no earthly thing."

—James M. Houston

NOTES

[1] Ecclesiastes 3:11.

[2] C. S. Lewis, *The Weight of Glory* (Greensboro, N.C.: Unicorn Press, 1977), p. 10.

[3] C. S. Lewis, *God in the Dock*, Walter Hooper, ed. (Grand Rapids, Mich.: Wm. B. Eerdmans, 1970), pp. 200–207.

[4] Quoted in G. F. Barbour, *The Life of Alexander Whyte* (New York: George H. Doran Co., 1925), pp. 117–18.

[5] Quoted in Richard L. Greeves, *John Bunyan* (Grand Rapids, Mich.: Wm. B. Eerdmans, 1969), p. 16.

[6] F. J. Sheed, ed., *The Confessions of St. Augustine* (New York: Sheed & Ward, 1949), p. 164.

[7] Ibid.

[8] Steven Ozment, *The Age of Reform 1250–1550* (New Haven, Conn.: Yale University Press, 1980), p. 239.

[9] Robert G. Tuttle, *John Wesley: His Life and Theology* (Grand Rapids, Mich.: Zondervan, 1978), p. 58.

[10] Ibid., p. 100.

[11] Ibid., p. 65.

[12] Earnest W. Bacon, *Spurgeon: Heir of the Puritans* (Grand Rapids, Mich.: Wm. B. Eerdmans, 1968), p. 108.

[13] C. H. Spurgeon, *Commenting and Commentaries* (London: Banner of Truth, 1969), pp. 2–4.

[14] Richard Baxter, *Practical Works,* William Orme, ed. (London: James Duncan, 1830), 4:266.

[15] Ephesians 3:20.

[16] C. S. Lewis, *God in the Dock*, pp. 200, 201.

[17] A. G. Sertillanges, *The Intellectual Life* (Westminster, Md.: Christian Classics, 1980), pp. 152–54.

[18] Soren Kierkegaard, *Purity of Heart Is to Will One Thing* (New York: Harper & Row, 1954), p. 184.

[19] Ibid., p. 193.

[20] Ibid.

[21] Carlos Carretto, *Letters from the Desert* (London: Darton, Longman, Todd, 1972), p. 32.

[22] See John Owen, *Sin and Temptation*, James M. Houston, ed. and J. I. Packer, cont. ed. (Portland, Ore.: Multnomah Press, 1982).

[23] Jean Leclerc, *Contemplative Life* (Kalamazoo, Mich.: Cistercian Publications, 1978), p. 109.

[24] Quoted by Leclerc, *Contemplative Life*, p. 117.

[25] Ibid., p. 116.

[26] John Owen, *Sin and Temptation.*

[27] G. F. Barbour, *Life of Alexander Whyte*, p. 378.

[28] Ibid., p. 389.

[29] Bernard of Clairvaux and his friends, *The Love of God*, James M. Houston, ed. (Portland, Ore.: Multnomah Press, 1983), pp. 233–51.

[30] See for example Richard Baxter, *The Reformed Pastor*, James M. Houston, ed., and Richard D. Halverson, cont. ed. (Portland, Ore.: Multnomah Press, 1982).

[31] C. S. Lewis, *God in the Dock*, pp. 201–202.

[32] Quoted by Roger Pooley, *Spiritual Autobiography* (Bramcote, Notts.: Grove Books, 1983), p. 6.

[33] Joseph Hall, *The Works* (London: M. Flesher, 1647), p. 114.

[34] Bernard of Clairvaux, *The Love of God.*

[35] William Wilberforce, *Real Christianity*, James M. Houston, ed., and Sen. Mark O. Hatfield, cont. ed. (Portland, Ore.: Multnomah Press, 1982).

[36] Jonathan Edwards, *Religious Affections*, James M. Houston, ed., and Charles W. Colson, cont. ed. (Portland, Ore.: Multnomah Press, 1984).

[37] David Lewis, ed., *The Works of St. John of the Cross* (London: Thomas Baker, 1891), pp. 586, 603.

SUBJECT INDEX

READERS' GUIDE

FOR PERSONAL REFLECTION OR GROUP DISCUSSION

READERS' GUIDE
INTRODUCTION

The Reformation began at that turning point of history in the West, which moved from a medieval to a modern frame of mind. Since it was a major event, its analysis is more complex than first meets the eye, so historians are still contributing new insights about it. Today, we are facing a similar order of magnitude of change, so we can gain perspective about our own cultural changes and religious challenges from studying the documents of this period. For it is only from historical reflection that we can be emancipated from the tyranny of the zeitgeist or spirit of the age we live in. For it is a mark of our arrogance that what is newest is "the best," so that for the Henry Fords "history is bunk." This spirit ignores that "every point of time is equidistant from eternity," or that "each epoch is immediate to God." So begin your discussion (with illustrations you experience), where to neglect the past is to secularize the present, personally or institutionally.

Rather we see that each period is the cradle for the next, so that the Renaissance did prepare for the Reformation, as the modern has now ushered in the "postmodern." "Crisis" is often a trigger-effect for change, so the Black Death of the mid-fourteenth century was analogous to the threat of a nuclear holocaust in the 1960s. The revival of Roman law reinforced the right to private property, as reaction to Roman law today has generated the feminist revolt with a woman's "right" over her own body and indeed her role in professional life. The revival of classical literature and learning we associate with the Renaissance renewed linguistic interest in the original texts, so that biblical scholarship in translation and exegesis prepared the way for the reformation of Christian doctrine. The new sense of human identity as "the thinking self" introduced by the humanism of Petrarch (1304–74), provided a new sense of individual consciousness in the Renaissance, which we see illustrated in Dante's Divine Comedy (1321). But having a "right relationship" with oneself, inevitably raised the question in a religious culture, how does one have a "right relationship with God"? The doctrine of justification thus became the focus of the religious consciousness of the Reformation. Today, individualism has become so excessive, like a cancer growth, that we may ask now, what crucial Christian doctrine needs renewed formulation for postmodernism?

GENERAL INTRODUCTION

In his book *The Reformation: Roots and Ramifications*, Heiko A. Oberman speaks of "three reformations in one epoch." First, there were the various efforts of conciliar reform in the fifteenth century, seeking to revise the nature of religious authority within the existing institutions of the church. Like the councils of the early church, the councils of Pisa, Constance, Basel, and Pisa (1409–1511) attempted but failed to bring about the desired changes. Are the contemporary constitutional struggles within mainline denominations attempting to repeat this approach? Second, there was the rise of the urban class of wealthy merchants, whose mobility and wealth propagated new independence of spirit, and actively engaged the publication and propagation of "reformed" literature. Was the independence of Geneva as a city-state the cause for the radical character of Calvinism? Is the "Christian in the marketplace" representative of a new renewal movement today? Third, there was the spread of refugees who entered a "new Exodus," and were conscious of being the godly "Remnant," spreading "salt and light" wherever they were. The Italian reformers were representative of this category, whether secretly within the Vatican itself, or more overtly so in cities like Naples, Siena, Florence, Bologna,

Padua, Modena, and Venice. But wherever the Reformation spread, the uniformity of its message was the same: by grace alone (*sola gratia*), by faith alone (*sola fide*), by Scripture alone (*sola scriptura*). Do we have such doctrinal uniformity today, with the Evangelical movement? Does the Reformation issue, "what must I do to be saved?" have the same urgency, and central concern with us today?

Part One: Juan de Valdés, The Experience of Justification by Faith

Chapter One

1. Commentators still struggle to define what is meant by humankind being created in the image and likeness of God. Can you improve on what Juan de Valdés has given us?

2. Contemporary humanism is usually atheistic, whereas the Italian Renaissance humanists were generally devout Christians, so why the contrast?

3. Discuss further on the issue of whether a nonbiblical view of our humanity can ever be fully human. Is that why the natural man can never fully understand his true identity?

4. If our goodwill is too weak to do God's will, how does the author suggest it can be done?

5. What are the four realities the writer describes of the new covenant?

6. How true are we to our baptism, if we interpret our relation to the flesh as weakly ascetic, and not as being dead to it?

Chapter Two

1. What we call natural reason is not always reasonable to others, but it is motivated by self-interest. How much more can our use of reason alienate us from God?

2. Juan de Valdés was aware that the relationship of knowing God was essential to knowing the truth. Are we as critical today, that an intellectual grasp of Scripture or theology may not derive from knowing God?

3. The text of Gensis 3:5 is ambiguous. The possible rendering is that knowing good and evil is the mark of being like God. Thus it is the temptation of Satan for human beings to be heroic, where the boundaries become blurred between the human and the divine (see Gen. 3:22). The serpent suggests that God prevents us from being fully human. Have you been tested to think that being a Christian cheats you from fully enjoying life to the full?

4. In the pursuit of happiness, how can knowing God truly bless you?

5. How does Juan de Valdés understand the role of doubt in the Christian's life?

6. It is commonly misunderstood that faith is a substitute for the absence of knowledge; rather both are relational terms like love and trust. So how does our faith grow with our knowledge of God?

Chapter Three
1. The absence of confessional faith in academic theology has been disastrous for the church. How does the author see the effects of the Holy Spirit within the life of the Christian, whether he is a scholar or not?

Chapter Four
1. How does the author elaborate on the passage of Romans 8:26?

2. What are the ten attitudes for true prayer that arise from meditation upon the Lord's Prayer?

Chapter Five
1. Curiosity was a much more serious vice to medieval Christians than we assess today. But our motives for Bible reading have not changed, so reflect on the statement of p. 51, "the occupation of a

Christian does not consist merely in an accumulation of knowledge but in a lived experience of it."

2. What are the seven reflections the author has concerning the Christian's use of the Scriptures?

Chapter Six

1. The Reformers were aware that their primary calling was to be godly. What we now term our *calling* professionally was only of secondary consideration. This is why the doctrine of justification was so much more central than in our contemporary consciousness. So is the commentary on vocation on pp. 58–64 of any relevance to the modern reader?

2. How does the author come to the conclusion that "Love gives taste and relish to sustain faith and hope"?

3. How does a Christian differ from a stoic, when facing suffering?

4. Spiritual aridity is the common lot of the Christian. How do we interpret and deal with it?

Chapter Seven

1. The Italian Reformers did not call themselves by any leading churchman. Rather they referred to themselves as living in "the benefits of Christ." What aspects of Christ's benefits do we live by today?

2. It is still popular today, as in Mel Gibson's film rendering of the crucifixion, to focus upon the physical sufferings of Christ. This was a very strong motive for popular devotion in the Middle Ages. Instead, Juan de Valdés focuses upon the meaning of the doctrine of atonement. In this your focus?

3. How differently would you identify your bases for satisfaction from what Juan de Valdés portrays on pp. 80–84?

4. Why is piety/devotion not so central in the Christian's life today, as it clearly was for the sixteenth-century reformers?

Part Two: Don Benedetto, The Assurance of Justification by Faith

Reread Dr. Leon Morris's introductory essay for his survey of this work, (pp. xxii–xxxiii). The focus of his own writings is upon the centrality of the Cross of Christ.

1. Can we ever explore the mystery of original sin deeply enough (pp. 97–99)?

2. What does Benedetto mean by the five offices of the Law (pp. 101–103)?

3. Forgiveness and justification are practically synonymous terms in Paul's epistles. Benedetto closely follows on the apostle's teaching, demonstrating that divine forgiveness depends wholly on Jesus Christ. What aspects of this meditation strike you particularly (pp. 105–112)?

4. The symbol of the church as the bride of Christ was very popular in the late Middle Ages, in association with meditations on the Song of Songs. But significantly Benedetto focuses upon the apostle Paul's usage of the metaphor, in the light of the Reformed doctrine of justification. How should the church today reflect upon being "the bride of Christ" (pp. 113–120)?

5. Calvin developed his apologia for the orthodoxy of the Reformers in the *Institutes,* by quoting extensively from the early Fathers of the church, to demonstrate the Reformation was not doctrinal innovation but renovation. Benedetto does likewise to explain some aspects of the doctrine of justification (pp.121–126).

6. Benedetto now uses the symbol of being clothed in Christ to further show we live under the benefits of Christ (pp. 135–141). Yet dependence upon Christ is only one aspect of it, for the other is, are we prepared to share in the afflictions of Christ also?

7. Christian assurance has often been a cause of distress to Christian believers. Do you think the remedies suggested for it by Benedetto are enough, or do we need to explore this further today (pp. 143–163)?